HITCHIN

More Glimpses of the Past

More Items from
Hitchin Historical Society's
Hitchin Journal

Selected and edited by

Simon Walker

Publication Data

First published in Great Britain in 2021 by Hitchin Historical Society
Copyright © Hitchin Historical Society

ISBN   978-0-9926162-6-7

The publisher has used its best endeavours to ensure that any website addresses referred to in this book are correct and active at the time of going to press. However, the publisher and the author have no responsibility for the websites and can make no guarantee that a site will remain live or that the content will remain relevant, decent or appropriate.

Every reasonable effort has been made by the publisher to trace the copyright holders of material in this book. Any errors or omissions should be notified in writing to the publisher, who will endeavour to rectify the situation for any reprints and future editions.

Front Cover: A painting by the late Hector Connell, dated 16 August 1971. Hector painted views of Hitchin like this one and was a familiar sight at his easel. He also produced prints in monochrome. [SLW]

Contents

Right: Gunner's Butchers some fifty years ago. On the left is Portmill Lane. Gunner's has gone – the building now houses a Marks & Spencer "Simply Food" store. (SLW)

Acknowledgements

In volume I of this series I said that it was difficult to acknowledge all the people who have helped in the preparation of this book. The items in this volume are for the most part more recent than last time, but the problem remains.

The North Hertfordshire Museum Service has been generous with material as always, I would like to thank them. Alan Fleck, who knows more about Hitchin than I do, helped in providing both information and images.

Thanks members of Hitchin Historical Society, especially Bridget and David Howlett, Pauline Humphries and Terry Knight for their wide knowledge of local events, places and history. Thanks to John Scorer for the initial proof reading.

John Lucas scanned a large number of Journals, producing them as PDFs that made it possible, though time consuming, to convert the text into a format in which I could manipulate it.

Finally Mike Clarke for all his work as Publication Officer of Hitchin Historical Society.

As always, in the end the responsibility lies with me, so you know who to blame if things go wrong.

Simon Walker

Above: Hitchin is well served by images of the past. From the 1860s onwards, photographers have made images of the town. This view is the Market Place, looking towards Sun Street, in the late 19th century. [North Hertfordshire Museum Service]

Introduction

As I embark on this second volume of selections from the Hitchin Historical Society's *Hitchin Journal*, we are all at worrying stage of the Covid-19 pandemic. I hope this project will last until the crisis is over; it has given me plenty to do so far, that's for sure.

I won't bore you with all the same material that appeared in the introduction of volume I, just the important bits.

From its inception in 1977 Hitchin Historical Society has produced publications for its membership. Over the years it has been called a *Newsletter* or a *Journal*, before settling into the current pattern of two *Newsletters* and two *Journals* each year.

Is all the information completely accurate? Unless I have noted otherwise, to the best of my knowledge, yes. Inaccuracies may exist, though we have tried to eradicate them, and in some cases added to a few articles.

Dates: the date that each item appeared is given at its head. Please bear this in mind for example when an anniversary is referred to, such as the centenary of the Hitchin Thespians – the article appeared in 2002; or Shopping in Hitchin 50 Years Ago from the same year – so you need to do some sums to work out how old they are now.

If you enjoy the book, who knows? You might decide to join the Hitchin Historical Society. It costs very little. Just go to **www.hitchinhistoricals.org.uk** and follow the links!

Finally, I would like to say that without a conversation with my friend the late Leslie Mustoe, and his encouragement, the books would probably not exist.

Simon Walker
July 2021

Right: A view of Bridge Street, thought to date from 1885. This part of the street hasn't much changed, though the pub – the Plough – has long since closed. Butcheries no longer hang carcases outside their shops anymore, which on the whole is a good thing! (North Herts Museum Service).

Contributors

So many people wrote pieces, or supplied pictures, memories or information that have appeared in the *Hitchin Journal*! Some still with us, others passed, others anonymous. I have included below all I was able to identify. As with Volume I – Hitchin, Glimpses of the Past, I have taken the easy option by listing them all.

Betty Abrey	Colin Dunham	Dr John Horton
Nigel Agar	Mrs Dunham	Phil Howard
Robert Ashby	Aud Eastham	Bridget Howlett
Anne Ashley Cooper	Lynda Elmy	David Howlett
Ann Barrington	Derrick Else	Chris and Trina Hubbard
Paul Bell	David Everest	Pauline Humphries
Jacky Birch	Andrew Fell-Gordon	Harold Hunt
Bryan Blackmar	Sue Fitzpatrick	Peter Ibbert
Deirdre Boggon	Keith Fitzpatrick-Matthews	Janet Jones
Bill Bowker	Alan Fleck	Doris Jones-Baker
Ken Boxall	Derek Fosdyke	Terry Knight
Barbara Boxall	Tony Foster	Eric Krieger
Mary Bradbeer	Jill Frampton	D T Larkins
Stephen Bradford-Best	Joy Franklin	Frank Latchmore
Harold Burnett	Daniel Freedman	Stanley Lee
Ken Burton	Pat Gadd	Tony Leone
Barbara Cade	M. Goldsmith	Brian Limbrick
Reg Cannon	Millie Grant	Lyn Lloyd-Smith
Roger Carvell	Brian Grant	John Lucas
Gerard Ceunis	Zena Grant	Colette Mudd
David Chalkley	Mr A Greville Young	Lionel Munby
Jerry Chase	Jill E Grey	Dora Newberry
P A Clark	Audrey Griffiths	Mrs M D Newman
Alan Clark	Dr Adrian Haigh	Clifford Offer
Ellie Clarke	Mrs Barbara Hall	Helen Parker
Shirley Davies	Sam Hallas	Fred Peacock
John Davies	Tony Hanscombe	Dr M Peel
Marshall F Dellar	E. J. Harrison	Kay Petrie
Fiona Dodwell	Don Hills	Maya Pieris
Scilla Douglas	Reginald Hine	Ron Pigram
Charles Duchenne	Chris Honey	Mrs Pond

Bob Prebble	Kate Thompson	Richard Whitmore
Terry Ransome	Arthur Thorning	Jonathan Wilkins
Rosemary Ransome	Gerry Tidy	Jean Williams
Phil Rowe	Simon Walker	J. J. Willis
Hugh Russell	Ben Ward	Henry Wills
John Scorer	Barry West	Terry Wilson
Richard Stephen	Gwendoline West	Brian Worbey
Don Studman	Linda Westwood	
Alison Taylor	Allan Whitaker	

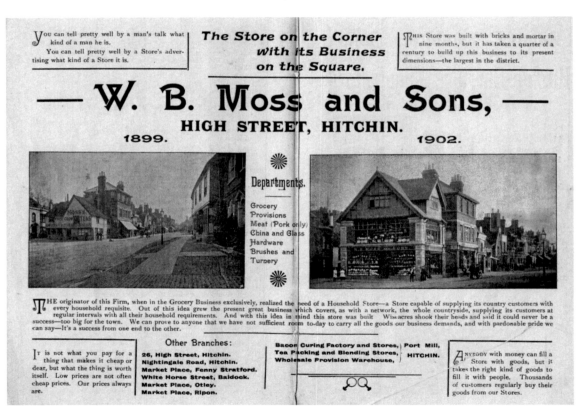

Above: W. B. Moss and Sons demolished their old premises at Moss's Corner (formerly the Troopers' Arms) in 1899. When this advertisement appeared in 1902 the new shop on the site had already opened. There were Moss branches in Baldock, Fenny Stratford, Otley, Ripon, and later Shefford. [SLW]

Vol 6 no 1, Spring 1987

My May Days

This first piece is a transcription of a recording by a member picking up the casual thoughts of an elderly lady in her eighties. Who the recorder was, and the interviewee, is unfortunately not recorded. It is interesting enough to be included here, I think. The period referred to then is between 1910 and 1920. SLW

'I don't know why you young people in the Historic Society don't try to re-enact all we used to do around May Day. I don't mean all this Labour stuff they talk about nowadays, but the real May Day Celebrations. Of course, it is well before your time dear, but I can remember it all so well. Same as Empire Day. Wonderful.[1]

I can remember my grandmother looking up from her washtub at the April skies. 'There won't be no May Day out for you girls,' she would say, all grumpy like. Of course, it seemed as though that made the skies go blue, and a few days later all the little girls round here would gather may blossom for May Day. The local grocer would carefully remove and save all the bands from the little butter tubs.

As the great day approached, we little girls would say to him 'Don't forget our hoops, mister'. He kept them almost up to the great day, and then each little girl would be given two. This was all we needed for the framework of a tiny chair which we made like a deck chair. Can you imagine it? We dressed our dolls up and placed them in the decorated chairs, and then on May morning we carried them round from door to door. All the grown-ups would get up early to see the 'May Girls' as we were called when we ran up to the doors.

When we formed the procession, all would be covered with may blossom and we also put violets, primroses (remember primroses before they all disappeared?) and perhaps some early bluebells on our chairs. We also carried bunches of May.[2] We had a little song but I'm sorry love, I forget it just at the moment. If I recall it I'll write it down.

Of course, we collected farthings and halfpennies and there was no nonsense about collecting for Oxfam or the Indians then - it all went straight into our pockets. The boys thought all this was silly, but we had the last laugh when we went round to the sweet shop afterwards. There weren't many at school that morning, I can tell you...

---

[1] Empire Day was first celebrated in 1902. It was in decline by the 1950s, and in 1958 was renamed British Commonwealth Day. It became simply Commonwealth day in 1966.

[2] May: Usually taken to mean Hawthorn, the white blossoms of which usually appear by the beginning of the month of May, hence the name; though it seems to appear early now, as a result of Climate Change. It is often thought to be the explanation of the saying, "Ne'er cast a clout till May be out." (Don't stop wearing warm underclothes until the Hawthorn is in flower.) Though May may refer to the month. The saying appears in Dr Thomas Fuller's "Gnomologia" published in 1732.

Hitchin - Railway Town

During the early years of this century, Hitchin seemed about to become a large railway centre when GNR proposed to move its Southern engineering and maintenance work to the town. Preparations were begun, but were abandoned with the start of WWI in 1914.

But Hitchin was still an important railway centre even before electrification and the daily commuter build-up at Hitchin Station, which suggests that local demand for rail services is ever increasing. Many of the railway people lived in the old Hitchin Queen Street area which was cleared under the slum improvement programme of the 1920s.

Above: Hitchin Goods Sidings and Station c.1933, from a contemporary postcard. The nearest sidings were for empty coaching stock, with the Benslow lime works sidings at the far end. The LNER (previously GNR) and LMS (previously MR) goods yards were to the left of the main line, in the distance, past the Cambridge Road underbridge (John Scorer).

Hitchin Station was the scene of several railway accidents. The Hertfordshire Express of 24th September 1932, records a typical incident which brought sorrow to the whole of the local railway community. Charles Barker, aged 64, was an engineer's labourer who lived in Telegraph Place. He was killed by a falling crane, the jury expressing an opinion that the bed upon which the crane stood was not strong enough to bear the weight. As they were lifting a four foot base of another crane from a railway wagon, something was heard to snap. There was a cry of 'For God's sake jump', but it appears that he did not jump quickly enough.

A nasty accident happened many years earlier on 21st July, 1888. The man who was killed was not a local man but a fireman from Doncaster. He was a victim of a straightforward railway accident. For some reason, although the signals were set against the train, the driver through some mistake kept the steam on, and the engine dashed against the side of the station signal box. The signalman and the driver of the train escaped without injury, but the fireman jumped clear of the train, but was caught between the train and the signal box wall and was killed instantly.

Perhaps the strangest railway case that I have come across recently happened to a Hitchin man who was found in a dazed condition in Barnet waiting room in 1883. Police were called and he was removed to Barnet Police Station where, gradually, his strange story came out. He was 32 years old, and had travelled up to London with his wife. She had left him at Holloway and he had gone on to meet a mysterious friend in Lombard Street. He refused to name the 'friend' but the man handed over to him 20 notes of £100 from the Bank of England. These he stuffed in his pocket and set off again by train from Moorgate to rejoin his wife.

As he got into the carriage at Moorgate, two other people, a man and a woman, also got in. Shortly afterwards he experienced a 'peculiar sensation'. He looked at the others and they just smiled back. He got to his feet and tried to open a window, but he was too weak to do so. He remembered nothing of what happened afterwards, except that when he got to his senses back in the police station all the notes, and some loose change he kept in his pockets, had gone.

The Police thought that it was a clear case of drugging by some narcotic fumes, but how it was done, and how they knew that he was carrying a large amount of money, remains a mystery.

Vol 6 no 2, Midsummer 1987

Town Improvements

From the Hertfordshire Express of June 13 1868

TOWN IMPROVEMENTS. - Conspicuous among the many architectural improvements recently made in the town, is the handsome and unique block of gabled buildings just completed by Mr. Shilcock, on the south side of the Market-square. It is in the 16th century half-timbered style, but the panels, which are of stained deal to imitate old oak, are herringboned with bright red bricks, instead of being filled up with plaster. The picturesque and striking appearance of the building heightened by the tasteful style in which decorative art is used, for purposes of utility.

Thus the roof is surmounted by a neat crest, and above the gabled end is a gilded vane with *fleur-de-lis*; while over the bay window of the upper block rises a French turret, covered with ornamental slates, and topped by gilded bannerets. In front are spaces for the reception of encaustic tiles.

Right: Shilcock's building in the southern side of Hitchin Market Place, centre, in the early 20th century. (North Hertfordshire Museum)

The one portion of the building is occupied by Mr. Boardman and his stock of china and earthenware. On the ground floor of the other portion are the offices of Mr. Shilcock, to whom the property belongs, and over his apartments is the *Express* Office, where we shall be glad in future to receive all personal and written communications on matters of business.

Vol 6 no 2, Midsummer 1987

Alternating Currents: Gas and Electricity in Hitchin

Following the sale of British Gas the electricity supply industry is the next big share sale expected. These public utilities have their origin in the nineteenth century energy explosion which spread through the towns of Great Britain. Their development in Hitchin provides a snapshot of the historical process.

William Murdoch made gas privately and lit his house at Redruth in 1792. Although some Hitchin citizens and firms were to manufacture their electricity privately at the turn of the century, the supply of gas and electricity to the community was a joint venture by citizens with the need for legislation to dig up roads, lay pipes and raise the money to do so.

In 1810 a bill to form a gas company laid before parliament was passed, with capital of £200,000. The Chartered Gas Light and Coke Co. was formed to light up London's streets beginning with Pall Mall. In 1819 the citizens of Hitchin sought to light the streets although the means is not stated. By 1829 there were 200 companies active in the United Kingdom. On October 25th 1830 the Workhouse in Bancroft was the venue for a meeting to 'consider the propriety and means of lighting the town of Hitchin with gas'. John Hawkins, the lawyer, chaired the meeting which resolved that a Company be formed and capital of £3,000 be raised by the issue of 150 shares at £20 each.

After the appointment of an engineer, Mr. George Lowe from the Chartered Gas Company, half an acre of Benge Mead was leased from the Trustees of Skynner's Charity for 99 years at £5 per annum.

Above: Olive Klaveren's photograph of the Bancroft Recreation Ground pond, in the winter of 1942/3. The Starlings Bridge gasometer in the background. Olive is second from the right, aged about 10. (Olive Klaveren)

The job of building the works, laying 4,000 yards of mains, 3,000 feet of service pipes and erecting 65 street lamps was given to Mr. West of Durham. The work was completed by 8th October, 1834 at a cost of £2170. Hitchin streets were lit and in the first year 161 lighting burners were installed in private premises. It was, however, a rich man's amenity with prices higher than those paid 130 years later. The profits for the first year £143.18s.1d. yielded a dividend of 5%. The project prospered so that after two years five new retorts replaced the original three. The coal used to produce gas had to be transported by road from the wharfs at Girtford and Biggleswade. This must have been quite an undertaking. As early as 1757 a plan had been included in an Act of Parliament to make the River Ivel and its tributaries navigable. This would ultimately have brought barges to Grove Mill Wharfs. The plan was overtaken by improvements in road construction and turnpikes. William Lucas the diarist noted in March 1814 winter coal was in short supply, there was none at Biggleswade and at Ware. 2s 6d was being asked. In November shortage of water in the canals again led to a shortfall in coal supplies. Meetings were held in 1824 and 1825 to extend the canal from Langford to Hitchin. At that time 6,000 tons of goods were transported annually by carters to Hitchin.

The gas produced was for lighting initially then for cooking. The price had come down but not until prepayment coin meters were introduced did gas spread to ordinary homes. The invention or the incandescent mantle replacing the fishtail or batswing bunkers gave another boost of popularity.

In 1895 there were 200 prepayment meters, for which the Hitchin Gas Company launched an advertising campaign. The number of prepayment meters doubled and so the following year land was bought in Walsworth. 1904 saw a new gasholder arise at a cost of £4,200.

Small scale nationalisation, or should it be urbanisation, was mooted in 1905, when Hitchin Urban District Council offered £33,250 for the Hitchin Gas Company.

The directors of the company turned the offer down and continued to prosper despite contingencies of war, and the 1926 strike. By 1932 the price of 1000 cubic feet was reduced to 3/9d. Now we enter the take-over phase.

In 1933 the Tottenham and District Gas Co. bought up Hitchin, Stevenage, Biggleswade and Shefford gas companies. Hitchin gas works gradually took over the production function of the other local concerns. All over the country small concerns were being taken over by holding companies like the British Gas Light Company, which took over Baldock. Old works needed modernisation which often meant closure. In 1937 the Tottenham Gas Co. bought 26 acres of land beside the railway off Cadwell Lane. The private ownership ceased in 1949 when Clement Attlee's government nationalised the industry.

In the same year Electricity was brought under state control. The Electric Lighting Act of 1882 discouraged the building of central power stations in Britain by limiting the rights of promoters to 21 years. Most early power stations, built in 1870's and 1880's were designed to supply individual premises such as the Gaiety Theatre and Billingsgate Fish Market in 1878. These early units were powered by Siemens steam generators. This equipment caused trouble and Dr. Sebastian Ziani de Ferranti was called in. He made radical changes and in 1887 a new company, The London Electric Supply Corporation was formed. This supplied power from Regents Park to the Thames and from Knightsbridge to the Law courts. Distribution was overhead cables fixed to iron brackets on housetops.

Its local beginnings were back in 1902 with the Hitchin Electricity order under the Electricity (supply) Act 1882 and Electric Lighting (Clauses) Act 1899. Hitchin Urban District Council like most other areas applied for new power. It was 1904 that the council leased the right of supply to the Electric Supply Corporation of London. Some local citizens already had their own generators to light their homes, the power being stored in wet cell batteries. Bert Wells, who died a few years ago, had one of these elegant contraptions in his West Hill workshop.

Whinbush Road was the site of an electricity generator, powered by the output of a small dedicated gas works.

Above: Hitchin Gasometer in the fog, with steam from a locomotive passing the gasworks at the end of Cook's Way, 2 February 1949. (Courtesy English Heritage)

On 1st April, 1906 the generators began putting out a new energy source, direct current to consumers, 240 volts for light and 480 volts for power.

The beginnings were hampered because the gas company was a local concern with townspeople as shareholders, whereas the electric company was private from outside. The main users of electricity were the Queen Street waterworks pumps and Hitchin Railway Station's water pumps for fitting train boilers. As the supply was often unreliable both major users working at once could, at peak times provoke a breakdown.

The population at large having accepted gas were reluctant to change.[1]

By 1918 there were only half a dozen experimental electric street lights. In the 1920's electricity became more popular but as consumers increased breakdowns of the ageing generators became more frequent. Only an agreement for topping up the supply from G W Russell and Sons Ltd.'s steam generating equipment kept the electricity running.

In 1923 the Hitchin Urban District Council refused permission for a price increase and the continuation of the electricity supply was threatened. Electrical Commissioners met at the Sun Hotel and gave the company two years to improve its performance. The Company offered an option to the Council to acquire the undertaking. This was taken up in July 1931, a month before the option ran out. The electricity undertaking was bought for £67,000 plus costs for HUDC.

In 1925 there were still 600 separate supply undertakings. The Electrical Supply Act of 1926 established the Central Electricity Board which had compulsory powers to concentrate the production of electricity at a relatively few stations, which could be depended upon to maintain an adequate load, at a standard alternating frequency. The board was also given the powers to construct a national grid which, for the first time, would collect up supplies all over Britain. It was then that the familiar galvanised pylons appeared on the face of the countryside.

Meantime in 1927 there were 570 consumers, the load was eased by taking bulk supply from North Metropolitan Power Co. Ltd. By mid-1928 the Whinbush Road generators had closed down.

Hitchin Urban District Council held electrical supply control for 18 years and by nationalisation there were 5,000 consumers. Electricity gradually took over street lighting from 1937/38 onwards.[2]

And so the wheel goes round except that the workhouse is unlikely to be the place for launching privatisation.

---

[1] Derek Fosdyke reported that when electricity took over from gas for lighting his house, it was noticeably colder to live in.
[2] There were still gas lamps on Elmside Walk in the late 1950s. [SLW]

The Hitchin British Schools

Yesterday and Today

Above: The Hitchin British Schools buildings. The building on the right is the headmaster and headmistress's houses. [SLW]

We hear much today about tailoring education to useful ends, about teaching children quickly and efficiently and about the need to fit the nation's youth for their place in a modern economy. None of these concerns is new. As the factory system revolutionised British manufacturing capability from the mid-eighteenth century, so interest grew in improving education for the masses, so that ordinary people could cope with the huge changes confronting them, contribute to the evolving economy and find their religious beliefs. From the 1780s the Sunday School movement gathered pace but England and Wales, unlike Scotland, lacked the basis of a national system of elementary education.

13

In 1798, however, Joseph Lancaster, a Quaker, opened a small school in Southwark, South London, in which he claimed to educate children in a new way. Lancaster instilled a sense of discipline and used the slate and pencil to teach children basic literacy and numeracy.

Most importantly, he borrowed from Dr Bell, an Anglican clergyman, the idea of teaching by 'monitors', almost the educational equivalent of a factory system. The 'monitorial system' was soon dubbed 'the steam engine of the moral world' and 'worthy to stand parallel and rival to the most useful modern inventions in the mechanical departments.'

The whole edifice depended on the schoolmaster being assisted by a number of the older and more able pupils who each worked under his supervision to teach a group of about ten children. In this way 'one master could teach a thousand boys' because 'what a boy can learn, a boy can teach'. Even better, a thousand children could be taught for less than £300 per year; costs usually fell between 5s.0d. and 7s.6d. per head per year.

This new method of teaching determined the main features of school construction, and early monitorial schools were usually in the form of a single room.

Elementary education, apart from providing instruction in reading, writing and arithmetic, was also to be morally corrective. After all, the movement had grown up not only during the upheavals of industrialisation but also in the shadow of the French Revolution - social stability was as important as economic utility. Reading material was specially tailored to this end. For example, a contemporary text exhorts:

> 'James Johnson was a good boy and loved learning. On Sundays when other boys were engaged in evil sport, he would turn aside from them and go to school early. James Johnson lived to be a happy man.'

Very many Quakers were interested in philanthropy and good works at this time and Lancaster succeeded in interesting many co-religionists in his system. He also developed aristocratic patronage and eventually received support from the King himself. His ideas were also studied by some of the foremost political thinkers of his day; Jeremy Bentham and John Stuart Mill pondered the possible extension of his methods for secondary education.

By 1805 the Southwark School had grown to 1000 pupils, and in 1807 the Royal Lancasterian Society (RLI) was formed to offer non-denominational education on a national scale. The Church of England also followed suit, establishing its own National Society in 1811. Interest in monitorial methods was also increasing abroad.

Lancaster was, however, a poor manager and soon found himself in financial difficulties which contrasted starkly to normal Quaker prudence. In 1814, after a period of increasing friction, he parted company with the Institution, eventually emigrating to the United States, where he died in 1838. The RLI transformed itself into the British and Foreign School Society, which explains today's references to Hitchin's 'British' schools.[1]

Hitchin, then North Hertfordshire's most important centre, was an early beneficiary of these educational advances. Lancaster himself visited the town in 1808, and, two years later, the Independent William Wilshere and Thomas Brand (later Lord Dacre) endowed a school in Dead Street (now Queen Street), the first of its kind in Hertfordshire.

Originally the intake was restricted to boys but, in 1819, under the influence of Curate Joseph Niblock, of St Mary's Church, provision for girls was also made. Following Wilshere's death in 1824, both schools were placed in the hands of twenty Trustees, half non-conformists and half Anglican.

The popularity of the school in a town with many aspiring artisans and trades people was soon apparent. By 1835 instruction was being given to 195 boys and 106 girls and overcrowding had become a problem.

At the national level, government had now recognised the value of voluntary educational effort and some central funds were available to top up local enterprise. In 1836 the Queen Street Trustees became early beneficiaries of this largesse when they received a building grant of £175. Attitudes to public spending have also changed little because they had, in fact, asked for £250 and the final expenditure was over £900. The grant was, nevertheless, a significant increase on the £72 initially offered and was a major boost to the school's development. It enabled a proper Lancasterian teaching room to be erected sufficient for a master, thirty monitors and three hundred boys. This room still exists today and is the only such survivor anywhere in the world.

Fire destroyed the original buildings inhabited by the school, latterly used for infants and the girls, in 1845 and by 1847 the Trustees had accepted supervision by government inspectors to improve provision further.

In 1856, therefore, further expenditure was authorised for a new school building to house infants, girls and boys. Interestingly, the inspector involved in forming the new plans was Matthew Arnold, and his suggestions resulted in the galleried classroom of 1853, another very rare surviving feature of the site.

These mid-Victorian developments allowed the demolition of what remained of the old seventeenth century accommodation and the erection of two purpose built dwellings for the school master and school mistress, completed in 1857. At the same time, William Wilshere, jnr., nephew of the founder, gave two hundred books as the nucleus of a school library.

---

[1] The British School in Queen Street was not the only one in the area – Walsworth School, established in 1852, also taught under the RLI method. The building is now Walsworth Community Centre.

Apart from some small scale Edwardian 'modernisation' the structure of the site has remained virtually unaltered since 1857, although its place in the educational hierarchy has changed.

In 1929 much of the school's elementary instruction was transferred to the newly built Wilshere Dacre School. Elementary education did continue in Queen Street, however, until this too ceased in 1969. From then until its recent closure the site was used for various further and adult educational purposes and, of course, as home to part of the Jill Grey Educational Collection. The site was listed Grade II in 1975.

Today the Hitchin British Schools Trust is in the process of raising £2m. to safeguard this unique piece of British educational history and to provide a home for the Jill Grey Collection, which itself is of national importance as a collection of school text books and other educational material.

A Friends of the Hitchin British Schools Museum has also been established and was officially launched on 16th May 1992 at Hitchin Town Hall. Many members of the Society have already become involved with the work of the Trust and Friends.

If you are interested in helping, or just in finding out more about what is going on, further details can be obtained from:

British Schools Museum
41/42 Queen Street
Hitchin SG4 9TS
Telephone : 01462 420144
admin@britishschoolsmuseum.org.uk

Vol 7 No 1, Spring 1989

As mentioned above, the Hitchin British Schools Museum, Queen Street, is the custodian of the Jill Grey Collection, which consists of some 37,000 items relating to the history of education and the social history of childhood. The Museum's website says:
"Jill, a Hitchin lady, amassed her unique collection between 1962 and 1987 and has a remarkable story to tell.
"An eccentric yet extraordinarily gifted woman, Jill Grey (1919 – 1987) was a code and cypher officer with the Royal Air Force during World War 2. After the war she went to the USA as personal assistant to Air Commodore Sir Frank Whittle, inventor of the jet engine, at a time when American companies were negotiating to use his important invention.
"During the 1950s she began to collect all things associated with early education and childhood – eventually completely filling her house in Hitchin with books, postcards and items of furniture, costume and much, much more.

"In 1975 she succeeded in getting the buildings at the British Schools in Hitchin 'listed', so confirming their architectural importance and helping to protect them from future demolition. She opened a small museum in the Gallery Classroom, engaging visitors to our educational heritage."

The Jill Grey Collection

Fiona Dodwell

I had no idea when I started my job at the end of October last year just how vast and diverse this collection was. The range of this collection is enormous, and illustrates every aspect of children's education. I never know when I open up paper bags and unwrap newspaper quite what I am going to find!

Before Christmas I was working at The Priory School cataloguing books - 2,300 so far. My boss, John Marjoram, came several days to help me, and we went through all the boxes stored at the school to sort out what exactly there was. Some items not relevant to the collection have been returned to the family, and others removed to Queen Street. This is where I have been working since Christmas, sorting and cataloguing objects, costume, ephemera, post cards and photos. There was enough money available to buy some conservation boxes, which means items can be stored properly and kept dust free.

As it is now easier to find things, we were able to loan items to the Hertfordshire County Council Centenary Year Exhibition and also to put on a small exhibition at Wilshere Dacre School as part of their 60th Anniversary Celebrations.

Whilst going through the boxes at the Priory School we found Jill Grey's accession books (listing the items she collected - Ed.) which go up to number 13,1027 covering ephemera, post cards, photographs and objects. Books are separate, and I should guess that there are well in excess of 14,000. There are still about 100 boxes to come from Pauline's cellar.

When the collection has been catalogued and room has been found to store it, I am sure it is going to prove a marvellous resource to a wide range of people.

[I asked Pauline Humphries if she remembered this – she replied as follows: "Hi Si, Yes, this is me! Following Jill's death her house in West Hill was sold and the Collection (which comprised multiple boxes of material) was divided for storage between Jean Williams' barn in London Road and our cellar in West Hill… Fiona was employed to 'sort it out' and catalogue it. For a time she worked in a screened-off area in my Library at (the then) Hitchin School, before moving with it to larger premises at either Wilshere Dacre or Oughtonhead School. Our cellar had only been partially cleared but was good for storage as temperature-controlled and quite dry. They don't build houses like that nowadays!" SLW]

Vol 8 no 2, May 1992
[The following article is not for the faint-hearted, but it reflects how butchers functioned not so many years ago.]

F. W. Coopers, Butchers, Tilehouse Street, 1937-41
By Marshall F Dellar

I started my working life at Meredews Furniture Manufacturers in Letchworth.[1] My main job was using a buffing wheel and polishing out the scratches on glass before it was silvered and made into mirrors. I was happy doing this work but mother was most unhappy as my clothes were permeated with rouge, a bright shade of red and this made everything else in the wash the same colour. Mother persuaded me to leave Meredews and try my hand at some other vocation.

There were two jobs on offer, firstly as a dentist's assistant and secondly as a butcher's boy. You've guessed it - I chose the butcher, having an inbuilt hatred of dentists!

My first day working at Coopers, as far as I can recollect, was a morning spreading sawdust on the shop floor, using emery cloth to clean the shop rails (no stainless steel in those days) and then sent out with meat to be delivered to Wellbury School between Offley and Pegsdon. Those errand boys' bikes were hard work and heavy going to a fourteen year old.

In the afternoon I would be set to work in the slaughter house or holding on to a rope passed through a hole in the wall with an irate bullock on the other end prior to being shot with a humane killer. Next job would be shovelling up all the mess in the slaughter house and transferring it to the muck heap in the yard.

Other jobs I had to do was to feed and water the pony, named Daisy, in her stable, give her clean bedding, etc. She was used to ferry a Mr. Arthur Knight on his rounds, delivering and collecting orders for meat and offal. Deliveries were on Tuesdays, Thursdays and Fridays. There were several hostelries served with meat, etc.; the first was *The Greyhound* at St Ippolyts, a Benskin's house.[2] A glass of beer was always given to the driver of the horse and cart and a small glass to myself which was always given to the driver! Our next call on route was to another small pub in St Ippolyts village on the hill, *The Olive Branch*, long since closed.

Our next call was, you've guessed it, *The Buck's Head*, at Little Wymondley, then onward to our next and last call, *The Green Man* at Great Wymondley. Here outside was a triangular piece of grass, still there today. Daisy, the pony, would stubbornly refuse to budge until she

---

[1] Meredew was taken over by Stag of Nottingham; manufacturing closed in 1990.

[2] Another pub that's closed down – one of many I've been in that are no more. One day I'll make a list... Benskins was taken over by Ind Coope in 1957. This in turn was part of a merger as Allied Breweries in 1961. Allied Breweries merged with J. Lyons and Co to form Allied Lyons; the breweries business merged with Carlsberg in 1992 as Carlsberg-Tetley, now part of Carlsberg Group. SLW

had had a feed from the sweet grass thereon. Meanwhile, Arthur and I would have our lunch break in the public bar helped down, no doubt, with a further glass of ale.

On returning from making deliveries our next job would be down in the cellar beneath the shop where preparations would be made for making sausages for sale in the shop. At 5.30pm the shutters had to be got in from a cupboard inside the yard gates and affixed to the shop windows. (Note: original windows and tiles (ceramic) are still in situ.)

Tuesday was a big day - Market Day. The van had to be loaded up with meat, scales, knives, steel, wrapping paper (newspaper) and all transported down to St Mary's Square where the market used to stand. A great quantity of meat and sausages would be sold from an open market stall, which I'm sure would not be allowed today.

Back at the shop things were happening in a big way. Maybe a large consignment of bullocks – Pole Scots (small black scotch bullocks from Scotland) or maybe twenty or thirty huge Hereford bullocks with enormous horns would arrive. They would be accommodated in a large bullock pen in a meadow at the top of the yard.

Pigs would be put in small sties in an outhouse in the shop yard prior to slaughter. Sheep would be delivered by large lorries and taken round to a meadow in Wratten Road or to a meadow at the top of Offley Road called Moormead Hill. They would be collected as and when required. Looking back, I must be the last person still alive to have driven sheep from the top of Offley Road or Wratten Road to the shop in Tilehouse Street. One of us would walk in front and the other behind and try and walk them steadily to the shop. On arrival the person in front would get hold of the nearest sheep and pull it up the yard and the rest would all follow.

Mr.Frank Cooper, the eldest of the Cooper brothers, ran the shop and slaughter house in Tilehouse Street. He had three brothers and one sister. Brother Ted ran a butcher's shop in Baldock, always a nice trip when we delivered his meat. Brother Wally, the youngest, kept a shop in Bancroft next to the Regal Cinema, and now a fish shop. Another brother, George, was not a butcher but a greengrocer in Welwyn. The sister, named Minnie, lived in Upper Tilehouse Street, at No.66, I believe.

I have mentioned various activities that went on at the shop but perhaps the one thing that stands out most in my mind was Thursdays, a big day. The brine tubs would be searched for hocks of pork, odd pieces of beef, etc. All would be boiled up for most of the day, cooled and then all bones removed, meat minced, herbs and spices added mixed with juices they were boiled in, poured into large bowls and allowed to set overnight to be sold as brawn the next day at about sixpence a pound (2 ½p).

Also a day remembered by many of the older generation was 'Faggot Day'. Pigs' liver, ox liver, lights, hearts, bacon and salt pork were all minced up. Bread and rusk, a kind of biscuit crumbs, were added and all mixed together and placed in large square baking trays, marked and shaped and pigs' fat spread over the top. They were then carried to the top of Tilehouse

Street to No.70 (Mr Hidgecock, the Bakers) and baked in the baker's oven. They were then taken back to the shop where people would be in a queue with their basins etc. to collect the faggots which cost a few pence each. They were known far and wide.

A well-known story and true is that a chauffeur-driven car would come all the way from the London area and often the lady's voice would call to the chauffeur "Don't forget the gravy, Henry."

As I grew older and more experienced, I joined other staff in more work in the slaughter house etc. To my delight I was also taught to drive the van, and used to drive Arthur on his rounds when the weather was not suitable for Daisy and the cart. The van used to behave just like the pony; it would not go past the *Green Man* until we had been fed and watered!

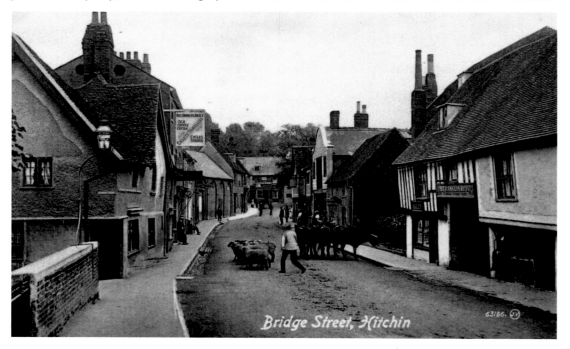

Above: sheep and cattle being driven down Bridge Street, in a contemporary postcard, registered in 1909. [SLW]

Saturday was pay day. After the shop had been swept, the chopping block scraped and everything cleaned up for the weekend, we would all be paid our wages. My share was about One pound and ten shillings (£1.50). I would then take Mr Cooper to his home in Bedford Road (No.75) where he used to live, not far from his beloved football ground or top field as it is now known.

In his younger days Frank played in goal for Hitchin Town Football Club, known then as Hitchin Blue Cross. He was a very good keeper as narrated by many an old Hitchin worthy who knew him in his younger days. After I had taken him home I would return the van to the shop, lock up the gates and go home, sometimes with an extra 5/- or 10/- (25p or 50p) for driving the boss home nightly.

Right: one of the two ceramic tiled panels at no.78 Tilehouse Street.   Below – a close-up showing more detail.   [SLW]

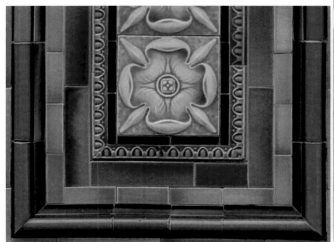

My story ends now as in late 1941 I volunteered for the Royal Navy where I served until demob in 1946. Three months on the 'Sheffield', a cruiser, and four years in submarines.

Mr.Cooper passed away during the war years so I had no job to return to. I changed my uniform for that of a postman for the next thirty years, but that's another story.

Vol 8 no 3, September 1992

The Great Fire of Potton 1783: The Hitchin Connection
Peter Ibbert

During the summer of 1992 a group of members were guests of the Potton History Society and enjoyed a fascinating afternoon learning about this interesting Bedfordshire town. Our tour included an account of the Great Fire of 1783 and, as a record of Hitchin's contribution to restoring the damage (second only to that of London). Peter has kindly allowed The Hitchin Journal *to reproduce his notes prepared for the talk he gave the Society in April 1992.*

"The Gentlemen's Magazine of August 1783 carried the following report:-

'From Bedford - That on the 14inst. a small hay stack taking fire about the middle of the day, set the whole town of Potton in flames, which burnt for nearly four and twenty hours before it was extinguished. The damage is said to amount to £50,000, very little of which was insured. There were two engines, but so much out of repair as to be of little use.' Later accounts lessen the damage.

In fact the committee set up to raise funds for the 'Sufferers' received claims for £25,625; a considerable sum in those days when an average labourer might expect to earn around £30 a year. The committee raised over £5,000 in just over 11 weeks and published a 76 page document listing all donations and its distribution of the money. An impressive achievement for a town of around 1000 people in a low wage rural area.

The accounts list £269 as the expenses for collecting money from two collections. Donations were collected from towns from Manchester to London and Birmingham to Swaffham.

The £6,285. 6s. 5d. came from:-

Private Subscriptions	33%
Hertfordshire	17%
Hunts/Cambs	7%
London Donations	25%
Bedfordshire	11%
Other Counties	8%

The towns that donated the most were

1. Hitchin	£270	2. Bedford	£165
3. Biggleswade	£123	4. Royston	£114
5. Ware	£104	6. Baldock	£100

The committee did its job efficiently and used only 5% of the money for its expenses, distributing 95% to the 'sufferers'. The claimants consisted of 51 Traders and Farmers, 14 Labourers, 37 Servants, 14 Widows, 2 Minors and 1 Vicar.

In the end 15 individuals were allocated nearly 70% of the money collected and 76 townsfolk were given a total of £355 (5% of the total). This reflected the economic structure of the town, with a few prosperous farmers and traders, and many with little to claim for other than a few personal possessions.

The money from Hitchin helped in the rebuilding of the town. Its market soon revived, but the development of the A1 enabled Biggleswade and Sandy to expand and the Market Square saw a slow but steady decline in its prosperity, until its final demise in the first half of this century.

A number of buildings in King Street and on the Market Square date from the Fire and stand as a reminder of the generosity of the people of towns such as Hitchin who helped Potton in its darkest hour.

THE GREAT FIRE OF POTTON 1783
THE HITCHIN CONTRIBUTION
12th Sept 1783. First Subscription

John Radcliffe, Esq	£21. 0s. 0d.
The Rev.Mr Morgan	£4. 4s. 4d.
John Everitt, Esq.	£7. 7s. 0d.
Mr Richard Tristram	£7. 7s. 0d.
Mr William Wiltshire	£2. 2s. 0d.
Mr. Isaac Sharpless jun	£10. 0s. 0d.
Mrs Crabb	£2. 2s. 0d.
Mr Rudd Wheeler	£2. 2s. 0d.
Mr Isaac Sharpless sen	£5. 5s. 0d.
Mr Isaac Gray	£7. 7s. 0d.
Mr James Whittingstall	£2. 2s. 0d.
Mr John Collison	£2. 2s. 0d.
Mr Daniel Chapman	£2. 2s. 0d.
Mr Thomas Caporn	£2. 2s. 0d.
Mr Daniel Nash	£2. 2s. 0d.
Mr William Lucas	£7. 7s. 0d.
Mr Jos Wheeler	£7. 7s. 0d.
Mrs Simpson	£5. 5s. 0d.
Mr John Barron	£5. 5s. 0d.
Mr Thomas Evans	£5. 5s. 0d.
Mr Bristow	£3. 3s. 0d.
Mr Jos Pierson	£7. 7s. 0d.
Mr Henry Whittingstall	£3. 3s. 0d.
Mr Weston of Chalton	£2. 2s. 0d.
Mr Jos Ransom	£5. 5s. 0d.
Mr Richard Croft	£3. 3s. 0d.
Rev Mr Dove, Lilley	£2. 2s. 0d.
Mr Wabey	£2. 2s. 0d.
Mr Lyles	£2. 2s. 0d.
Mr Times	£2. 2s. 0d.
Mrs Berry	£2. 2s. 0d.
Mr Matthew Foster	£3. 3s. 0d.
Mr Field, Silsoe	£2. 2s. 0d.
Mr Bevans, Chicksands	£2. 2s. 0d.
Mr John Crabb	£3. 3s. 0d.
Mr Robert Thomas, jun	£2. 2s. 0d.

Mr Dimsdale, Surgeon	£2. 2s. 0d.
Mr Wiltshire, sen	£2. 2s. 0d.
Mr George Whittingstall	£2. 2s. 0d.
Mrs Ewsden	£1. 1s. 0d.
Mr George Paternoster	£1. 1s. 0d.
Mr Michael Foster	£1. 1s. 0d.
Mr Robert Thomas, sen	£1. 1s. 0d.
Mr Atkinson	£1. 1s. 0d.
Mr Churchill	10s. 6d.
Mrs Brandrith	10s. 6d.
Mr William Chapman	£1. 1s. 0d.
Mrs Field	£1. 1s. 0d.
Miss Field	10s. 6d.
Miss Deborah Field	10s. 6d.
Mr Button, sen	£1. 1s. 0d.
Captain Saban	10s. 6d.
Mr. William Bowers	10s. 6d.
Mr Isaac Field	£1. 1s. 0d.
Mr Nathaniel Field	£1. 1s. 0d.
Mr John Wiltshire, jun	£1. 1s. 0d.
Mr Thomas Boffey	10s. 6d.
Mr Thomas Green	10s. 6d.
Mr Spavold	£1. 1s. 0d.
The Rev Mr Geard	10s. 6d.
Mrs Batt	10s. 6d.
Mr Thrussell	10s. 6d.
Mr John Moore	£1. 1s. 0d.
The Rev Mr Griffiths	10s. 6d.
Mr Inskip	£1. 1s. 0d.
Mr Dearmer	£1. 1s. 0d.
Mrs Taylor	10s. 6d.
Captain Luvington	£1. 1s. 0d.
Miss North	£1. 1s. 0d.
Miss Mailing	£1. 1s. 0d.
Mr Coulson	10s. 6d.
John Draycot, Clerk Mr Lucas	£1. 1s. 0d.
Mr Hovel	10s. 6d.
Mr Thomas Marsh	£1. 1s. 0d.
Mr Paternoster	10s. 6d.
Mr William Dunnage	10s. 6d.
Mr Hanscombe	10s. 6d.
Mrs Wabey	£1. 1s. 0d.
Mr Cloake of Camberwell	10s. 6d.

Mr Ralph Race	£1. 1s. 0d.
Mr Field, Pulanger	£1. 1s. 0d.
Mr Alberry	10s. 6d.
Mr Taylor, Holwell	£1. 1s. 0d.
Mr Barber, Perton	10s. 6d.
Mr Barber, Ashwell	10s. 6d.
Mr Inskip, Old Warden	£1. 1s. 0d.
Mr Taylor, Stanford	£1. 1s. 0d.
Jos Hutton,Ridgeway,Sheffield	£1. 1s. 0d.
Mr Crawley, Offley	10s. 6d.
Mr Thomas Williams	£1. 1s. 0d.
Mr Mugglestone	£1. 1s. 0d.
Young Gents, Mr Evan's School	£5. 5s. 0d.
Mr Barry at the Sun	£1. 1s. 0d.
Mr Dear	£2. 2s. 0d.
Other small Subscriptions	£8. 15s. 6d.

Sept 19th 1783 Second Subscription:

Mr Taylor Rumerick; Rev Mr Pears; Rev Mr Whitehurst; Mr Hill, Whitewell; Mr Ed Kitchiner, Chells; Mr Whitney; Mr Nicholls, Whitewell; Mr Massey; Mr Willingham; Mr Easy, Weston; Mr Pestell, Moppershall; Mr Barber, Broom; Mr Thomas Hailey; John Carrie Esq; Mrs Parr; Thomas Harwood Esq.	£38. 7s. 6d.
Other Small Subscriptions	£4. 11s. 6d.

(Spellings are as they appeared in the original, "Chalton" for "Charlton.")

As an interesting aside to the 1783 fire: another fire did great damage to the town in June of 1878. Amongst the details published in the Bedfordshire Mercury *was a paragraph that ran as follows:*

"In 1783 the greater part of the town which up to then had maintained a good market, was destroyed by fire, and since that time on several occasions has this awful visitant scared the townsfolk. A curious superstition of this part of the country, in common with much a larger area was verified by this fire. It is commonly believed that if a hare runs through the streets of a town a fire is sure to follow, and certain it is that on Tuesday last a hare did run through Potton, and it was certainly followed by a terrible fire. Many of the inhabitants were really alarmed by the unwelcome appearance of "Poor Puss" [a dialect name for a hare] and seemed to take the dread news of Wednesday as the naturally expected result." [SLW]

Two Contrasting Hertfordshire Christmases
circa 1840

The celebration of Christmas is older than the County of Hertfordshire itself. Even before the inhabitants were converted to Christianity the occurrence of the winter solstice and the turn of the winter had been marked by festivities.

Past Christmases, as now, were celebrated in different ways by different people. In 1838, William Lucas recorded that on 25th December, he 'attended the London Quarterly Meeting [of the Society of Friends, or Quakers] the great house filled but not so overflowing as I have often seen it, and as it was Christmas Day and everybody was able to attend, I could see in this proof of an extensive defection. Hannah Backhouse, the most prominent performer, her appearance dignified, a fine study for a prophetess in the face, form and drapery. Her pronunciation less singular than usual, her manner fervid and solemn, and her mother spirit stirring. She drew a rapid sketch of the rise and decline of our Society which had recently become a shell without a kernel, descanted on the paramount importance of faith, and in a few bold strokes laid before us the most important of our testimonies on war, oaths and priestly maintenance etc... Not being able to get off by any coach before the mail, all the others stopping on account of the day, I dined at Stafford Allen's in the good company of the Listers, Robert Harrard and H. Tuckett.' (extract, A Quaker Journal I, p.154).

In 1835, in Ware, one James Smith sampled a Christmas that fits in more neatly with our vision of what the late Georgian/early Victorian celebrations would have been like. He described it as follows:

'Not to have gone to church on Christmas Day, of all the good days in the year, would have been an inexcusable social solecism, as well as a breach of religious duty. The building was quite a spectacle. The pillars and arches, the galleries and chandeliers, the brass lectern and the carved pulpit, the antique font, and the very organ itself were masked with holly and ivy, bay, laurel, and other evergreens. The roomy old family pews, in which you could slumber so comfortably on hot drowsy Sunday afternoons in the summer time were filled with troops of children home for the holidays. The 'gentry' from the Park were accompanied by other 'gentry' from London, whose costumes were the admiration and envy of the less fashionable townsfolk. The services were more musical than usual, and Luppino, the organist, used to regale our ears with a grand 'Voluntary'... As to the sermon, it was short and sweet, genial and practical. There was the largest offertory of the year, and Meares, the Sexton, and Mrs.Meares, the pew-opener, used to stand at the entrance of the great porch to receive their annual donation from the worshippers. Outside there were friendly greetings innumerable, family enquiries,

26

invitations 'to come round in the evening', and an interchange of the compliments of the season. The keen frosty air seemed to be pervaded by an odour of roast turkey, and from the bakehouses there soon streamed forth a procession of working-men's wives carrying home the steaming Christmas joint. The afternoon and evening were devoted to social enjoyment, prolonged until far into the night; and next day, if the weather was favourable, every sheet of ice in the neighbourhood was populous with skaters...'

(Extract quoted *The Folklore of Hertfordshire*, Dr Doris Jones Baker, pp 176-7]

Vol 9 no 2, July 1993

How Well Do You Know Hitchin's Listed Buildings?

By the late nineteenth century, at the end of a century of unprecedented change, there was a growing realisation that some systematic record of our local history should be made. In 1897 the Victoria County History was established with the aim of recording that history, county by county, in England and Wales.

The buildings of the nation also came under scrutiny and, in 1909, a Royal Commission on Historical Monuments was appointed to "forthwith ..... make an inventory of the Ancient and Historical Monuments and Constructions connected with or illustrative of the contemporary culture, civilisation and conditions of life of the people of England-- from the earliest times to the year 1700, and to specify those which seem most worthy of preservation." The Commission Report for Hertfordshire was published in 1910 and is still a valuable source of information for local historians.

Interest in building history continued to grow and, after the Second World War, during which many historic buildings were lost, the Ministry of Housing and Local Government was given the statutory duty to compile lists of buildings of architectural or historic interest to which protections were applied in relation to rebuilding and redevelopment. The first Lists (hence the term 'Listed Building') were compiled in 1948-49 and have been refined and added to ever since.[1]

Eligible buildings are "graded" for architectural and historic quality along the following lines:

Grade I
The very best of our building heritage comprising only 1% of all the Listed Buildings in the Country. Hitchin has one such building, The Priory (although St.Mary's is classified A on the scale applied to churches).

---

[1] There are more than 200 listed buildings in Hitchin wards. They can be viewed on the website **https://historicengland.org.uk/listing/the-list/**

The Priory Hitchin. Herts.

Above: Hitchin Priory in 1861; this is one of the two grade I listed buildings in Hitchin. The other is St Mary's Church. (North Herts. Museum). Below: the Priory from the other side of the river Hiz (source unknown).

Grade II*

Particularly special buildings comprising about 4% of all Listings. Hitchin has several examples such as the Galleried Classroom in the British School and the Biggin.

Grade II

Historic buildings often "grouped" in terraces or streets comprising about 95% of all Listings. Hitchin has very many such buildings, mainly in the town centre core.

These days buildings do not have to be very old to qualify for Listing; a "thirty year rule" now gives much greater scope to include buildings which have acquired particular significance. For example, in Birmingham, a road of 1930s semis has been listed because they have survived relatively intact and "typify" interwar suburban building.

Since 1967 the protection of Listed Buildings has been supplemented by local councils having powers to designate Conservation Areas which place controls on what can be done to buildings and landscape features, whether they are listed or not, to preserve the overall "feel" and "look" of an area. Hitchin, of course, has an important conservation area based on its medieval town core, but also extending to include portions of the nearer suburbs and green spaces.

Some local councils also provide encouragement to property owners to pursue the highest standards in restoration and rehabilitation. The Hitchin Urban District Council initiated an Annual Civic Award Scheme and this has been continued by the present local authority. You will see plaques applied to winning buildings around the town; for example, No.32 Bridge Street has one.

The following website lists listed buildings in Hertfordshire: https://britishlistedbuildings.co.uk/england/hertfordshire#.YNHB5OhKglQ

Next time you are walking around the town look out for Listed Buildings; sometimes they are obvious (such as the Biggin) but other times much less so (such as No. 91, Woolgrove Road). Also, remember that it is up to those of us who live in and know the town, to suggest further candidates for inclusion on the Lists. Much work and determination are required and a case has to be made for the importance of the building concerned but Jill Grey proved that it <u>can</u> be done with her campaign to have the whole British Schools site listed Grade II and the Galleried Classroom as Grade II*.

[In addition North Hertfordshire District Council maintains a Hitchin Register of Buildings of Local Interest: https://www.north-herts.gov.uk/sites/northherts-cms/files/hitchin_register_of_buildings_of_local_interest_.pdf *This list does not offer the protection that formal listing offers, but "the district council in making a decision on the application will take into consideration the local interest of the buildings included on the register." SLW]*

Where I Lived on Arriving in Hitchin by Derek Fosdyke

It was towards the end of 1944, when my mother, elder brother and I arrived in Hitchin. We came from Enfield, North London, leaving my father behind as he worked in a munitions factory and was not allowed to leave. We had lived a life of "bomb dodging" in and around London throughout the war but my mother said, "When Jerry started throwing things at us (the V2) that we couldn't see or hear until it's too late, then it's time to up and leave." So we did. On arrival, we joined countless other people in the New Town Hall where we lived for a couple of weeks. We slept in the big hall where it was literally "wall to wall" camp beds, some even slept on the floor. We had our meals in the British Restaurant known to our younger readers as the Corn Exchange or Craft Centre.[1] We then started a tour of Hitchin living in various billets or lodgings.

The first was with an old lady who lived alone in Sunnyside, alone that is except for a big old dog which I shall never forget. It was fat, and I mean fat, and it must have had a disease because it had hardly any hair on its body and it smelt horrible. I don't remember anything else from that address. I was only eight years old and my brother was twelve, and I seem to remember one thing and not very much of another.

I remember quite a lot about our next abode, it was 47 Queen Street (now gone to make way for the new Queen Street), it's difficult to forget it as it is in nearly every old picture of the street. We lived with a Jewish family, Mr. and Mrs. Jackson, their son Billy and daughter Ruby. Ruby was the youngest and both were younger than my brother and I. The house had two rooms upstairs and two rooms downstairs. The Jacksons slept in the front bedroom and had to go through our bedroom to get to it, as the top of the stairs was in a corner of our room. I suppose by today's standards it would be one bedroom with a large landing. Our room had one large bed in it which the three of us slept in, and when Dad came down for the weekend (which wasn't very often) then the four of us slept in the bed "top to tail." I can also remember a greatcoat that served as a blanket.

There may have been other furniture in the room, perhaps a small chest of drawers, though I don't remember any. The greatcoat doesn't mean we were poverty stricken though we didn't have much. That was because of being on the move much of the time my parents had put everything in storage. Downstairs was no less cramped, the front door led into the front room cum diner cum everything else, then into the kitchen which comprised of a stone sink (water came from a tap outside the back door), small table, gas stove, a cupboard and

---

[1] In December 1941 the Corn Exchange was converted into a British Restaurant, to provide cheap and nutritious meals to augment the severe wartime rationing. It is said that it catered for up to 600 people a day.

the stairs which took up all of one corner. The privy was a 'sentry box' by the back door. The council emptied it once or twice a week - God willing!

I don't know what Mr Jackson did for a living but I know he used to take a stall on the market. He would go out for the day and when he returned he would have a couple of sacks full of shoes. They were all odds or seconds or perhaps even second-hand and Mr and Mrs Jackson would spend the evening trying to make pairs of shoes, or as near as possible. This was done by gaslight as there wasn't any electricity in the house. There weren't the styles and different materials in those days and it wouldn't be too difficult to match two shoes that would satisfy someone. After all, shoes, like everything else, were on ration and you had to give coupons to get a pair, always assuming you could get a pair and had the money to pay for them. Mr. Jackson would sell them on his stall on the market. Also, on the market you could buy old bicycle tyres, less the steel rims. People would cut up the tyres into strips and nail them onto the bottom of their shoes. This would make a serviceable repair.

Another thing Mr Jackson sold was DIY calendars. He would get a lot of pictures of people like Winston Churchill, Queen Elizabeth, or King George VI (the people were very patriotic in those days), or some nice landscapes the size of postcards. He would then cut glass to the same size. This he would sell with a reel of passe-partout[1] and a calendar. The glass was laid on the picture the passe-partout put around the edge and the calendar stuck on the bottom, a woollen loop was attached to the top and 'BINGO' one calendar. We three boys had half a dozen each for Christmas 1944, I don't know what Ruby had as she was too young to play around with glass. I think she was 5 or 6 years old. How we managed to keep all our fingers I'll never know, we lived dangerously in those days!

One of our pastimes when we lived at No.47 was to meet the Yanks when they came "home." Home for them (or rather their transport) was the 'new' market square. They would drive up in the late afternoon/early evening, park up their lorries and then make their way to their billets. As they walked off, us three boys (Ruby being too young for everything), together with our mates and other urchins would follow up close behind shouting "Got any gum chum?" They would, most times, open up a packet and throw it over our heads and we would scramble like mad to get a piece. We did alright for gum, there was an awful lot of Yanks for us to exploit. They would do their bit of exploiting by asking "You kids got any elder sisters?" We never knew why girls interested them and we were not likely to find out as my brother and I hadn't any sisters and Billy only had little Ruby. Sometimes if we were really lucky the Yanks would have us scramble for chocolate.

My mother at this time had a job as a cook at the Hitchin Girls' Grammar School. She had to work Saturday mornings and this was bath time for my brother and I. Mother would meet us at the door at a pre-arranged time and would usher us into a bathroom where we would

---

[1] In this context, a strong paper gummed on one side and used especially for mounting pictures.

take our weekly 'tub'. I don't suppose there are many boys who can say they took a regular bath in the Girls' Grammar School. (Goodness knows what the Jacksons did for a bath).

We then moved to Walsworth to lodge with a dear old couple (well they seemed old to a young lad like me), Mr & Mrs Leonard at No.5 Woolgrove Road, opposite the church and the hooded crucifix. This must have been quite tame and uneventful compared with 47 Queen Street. There was one event that happened about this time that brings a smile when I think of it. We (big brother and I and a couple of mates), heard of a bomber coming down over Weston way, and boys being boys, we set off to find it. We found it alright. I can't remember now if it was German or one of "ours."[1]

It was a complete wreck with ammunition scattered all over the place, so we helped ourselves to a few souvenirs. We have since learnt that what we took home was about a dozen cannon shells. When mother saw what we had, she said we must take them to a Home Guard man that lived up Orchard Road. So off we went again, knock, knock, knock on Mr. Home Guard's door. When he opened it and saw us with a couple of armfuls of cannon shells, he nearly had a blue fit. He wouldn't touch them but told us to take them to the bottom of the road and throw them in the river. This we did, but by now word had got around and after we had thrown them in there must have been 10-12 boys all paddling and searching in the mud to pull them back out again. I wonder what happened to our armfuls of "paperweights."

We left Mr and Mrs Leonard (I don't suppose they were sorry), to go to live in a cottage that my parents had rented. The war was now over and we had celebrated Victory in Europe and Victory over Japan days, but that is another story. My father was able to leave his job and he came to live with us in our new home at 48 Cambridge Road (later to be pulled down to make way for the Adult Education College.) It was the end one of a row of four that belonged to the estate of Major Anderson, situated diagonally opposite the Ship on the other side of the bridge.[2]

It was 2 up and 2 down, the same as 47 Queen Street, but because this used to be the senior coachman's cottage it had a wooden floor in the front room. The other three cottages had the red quarry tile flooring, as did 47 Queen Street.

Our new home was quite "up market". It had cold running water in the kitchen, and we boasted a flush loo, albeit in next door's garden! There was a block of four loos in the middle of the two centre back gardens. It could be a little inconvenient on a dark night with snow on the ground. There were no front gardens and the front door opened from the front room

---

[1] The crash was probably the collision of two US B17 bombers, 42-97182 and 42-102936, on 26 August 1944. All but four of the airmen were killed, as well as a woman evacuee and her child. The cannon shells would probably have been .50 Browning machine gun cartridges.

[2] The Ship was renamed in 2001, and became the Millstream, having fallen prey to the fashion for renaming pubs in the hope of increasing the number of customers (or discouraging unwelcome ones).

directly onto the narrow footpath, then onto the Cambridge Road (A505). Later, our front door was to become the only one of the four that had a window in it. Father was working for the Bacon Factory (alas, that too is gone now), and he got the firm's carpenter to come along and put a pane of glass in it. We also had a barn at the bottom of the garden as did the other three cottages and a communal bakehouse, though it had gone out of use before we moved there.

Above: the cottages Derek and his family moved into are on the left of this picture. Walsworth House is in the background.

We didn't have a bathroom and mother had left the school, but we all still had our weekly bath. We had a big tin washtub and water was heated in saucepans and kettles. Each tubful used to do two, either Mum and Dad or my brother and me. Later, we had an Ascot fitted, and with the aid of a rubber tube we ran hot water direct into the bath. On very cold bath nights the tub was carried into the front room in front of the old black open range. Also, on these winter nights, a steamer full of porridge was kept on the range all night ready for breakfast the following morning. All this for a rent of five bob per week (25p). Sometime later, we had electricity installed and the rent went up (I don't know by how much), and the house got colder. There's something to be said for gas lighting in the winter.

All the above took place between the middle of 1944 and the end of 1945.

A Hitchin Man's Contribution to Victory in 1918

Clement Bernard Norris was born in Hitchin and spent all his life there except for some three years (1916-1919) spent as a soldier in the British Army.

He was the son of Fred Norris, a carpenter, and Helen Norris. The early part of his life was spent in a cottage called Mount Pleasant which stood at the top of Pirton Road overlooking the town. It was a reasonably comfortable if modest habitation and it was set in surroundings which were idyllic for its four young occupants. On one side of the cottage lay a field which for many years was used for the cultivation of lavender and which appeared as a trademark on the products of a manufacturing chemist in Hitchin (Perks and Llewellyn). At the rear of the cottage was an area of woodland, vestiges of which can still be seen, in which the children were free to wander and play.[1]

Above: A postcard view of Mount Pleasant. A much photographed building, with cards produced in both monochrome and colour. (Gerry Tidy)

---

[1] Clement Norris's sister (Millie Grant née Norris) wrote about her childhood at Mount Pleasant and in Hitchin. See p. 159-167, *Hitchin – Glimpses of the Past*, the first volume of HHS *Hitchin Journal* articles.

This paradise was lost in 1912 when the family moved down the hill to a house in Wratten Road on the death of Clement's grandmother. He attended the British School in Queen Street and on leaving school was apprenticed as a baker and confectioner with Nott's bakery, then in Nightingale Road. After war service he worked for Hidgcock's in Tilehouse Street and Waldock's in Bucklersbury. His hours were long, as was then customary in the baking trade, and his duties included the making of bread and confectionery and also a delivery round to houses in the district. He died at his home in Lucas Lane in 1962.

Clement Norris was by all accounts a hardworking and unassuming citizen of Hitchin. He did not seek a prominent role in the affairs of the town, preferring to devote his life to his family and his work. He was a good amateur pianist and he was much in demand when the extensive Norris family gathered for their Christmas celebrations in the home of his parents, Fred and Helen. Those were the days (1920s-60s) when some families still found enjoyment in singing well-known songs round the piano and Clement was skilled in accompanying the vocal efforts of the oldest and the youngest members of the family - no matter how shy the latter. As one of those young children in the 1930s it was difficult for me to picture my kindly, gentle uncle as a fighting soldier, but I knew that he had been such for I had seen his name on a board in the vestibule of Hitchin Town Hall. On the board were listed those men of the town who had been awarded medals for bravery in the "Great War." The most illustrious name was that of 2nd. Lieutenant Young, V.C. Somewhere below was the name of Lance Corporal Clement Norris M.M. [Military Medal].[1] I was of course anxious to know how my uncle had won his Military Medal, but there was a general understanding in the family that "Uncle Clem doesn't like talking about the War" and even a child could understand why that might be.

Despite my interest, therefore, I hardly ever spoke to him of his experiences. He died in 1962 and in later years, when it was too late to gather information at first hand I came to regret a reticence on my part which might perhaps have been over punctilious. On the death of his widow in 1986 there came to light two of his army documents (Army Forms Z21 and AGZ500)[2] and on seeing these, resolved, at long last, to piece together such information as I could discover in order to learn something of his wartime experiences and in particular of the action which led to the award of the Military Medal. Thus began a lengthy learning experience for a very amateur military historian. It was to take me to the Imperial War Museum and finally on a journey to France during which I retraced the steps of a particular

[1] The Military Medal was established in 1916, and was awarded for "acts of gallantry and devotion to duty under fire" to non-commissioned ranks. It was discontinued in 1993, after which the Military Cross was awarded to all ranks.
[2] Army Form Z21 - Certificate of Transfer to Reserve on demobilization; Army Form Z 500 - Unit Register Card.

British battalion in the autumn of 1918 from Gommecourt, south of Arras, as far east as the Normal Forest and the River Sambre.

It was necessary first to ascertain when Clement served in the army and in which unit or units. Army Form Z21 revealed that he was "attested" on 8 February 1916 and it is presumed that this date may mark the commencement of his army service. There is some dispute as to whether he volunteered or was conscripted. His surviving sister, Mrs M B Grant, believes that he was conscripted but his surviving brother, Mr A V Norris, recalls a conversation in which Clement reported that he had joined "Kitchener's Army" because "everyone else is joining up." Clement was "attested" and that word was employed in a recruitment scheme introduced by Lord Derby soon after his appointment as Director of Recruitment in October 1915. Men of military age were invited to attest their willingness to serve when and if their age group was called up. A Military Service Act became law in May 1916 and thereafter military service became compulsory. Clement reached the age of eighteen in July 1915 and could presumably have volunteered then. The fact that he was attested in February 1916 suggests that he was prudent enough to wait upon events and to come forward at a time when it had become clear that compulsory service was inevitable. Unfortunately his demobilisation form (Army Form Z21) does not record when he was "Called up for service...." The space is left blank. Since, however, he was just over 18½, and unmarried, at the time when he was attested it is highly likely that he would have been called up for service very soon after that date and that he joined the army at the end of February 1916. According to the other available document, his Unit Register Card AGZ 500 (a document which covered movements in 1919 from unspecified staging camps to the embarkation camp – Boulogne -- on his way to demobilisation in England) his length of service at that time was 3 years 2 months. It is therefore presumed that the undated AGZ 500 was issued in April or May 1919.

AGZ 500 also states that he had completed 2 years 10 months service in the field. This would indicate that he received some four months training in England before departure for France (all his overseas service was on the Western Front) and that he had arrived there in June or July 1916. A period of four months may seem to be very short but it might well have been customary in 1916. It is not known where he received his military training but Mr A V Norris has in his possession a photograph which appears to be a typical "recruit" photograph of the sort newly-enlisted soldiers had taken in order to send to their families and this bears the address "Imperial Studios, 47, Union Street, Aldershot". This may be an indication of where some of his early days in the army were spent. The documents confirm that his service number, or Regt No., was 6670 and that at the time of his departure from active service in 1919 he held the rank of corporal in the Middlesex Regiment. His final contact with the Army appears to have occurred on 8th November 1919, by which time he must long since have returned to his home in Hitchin and his civilian occupation of baker. On that date he was issued with his "Certificate of Transfer to Reserve (Army Form Z21) His rank is given as Private which suggests that the rank of Corporal was a temporary one held on active service in France. Thus the very limited documentation so far available to me had at least furnished information on Clement's dates and length of service and on ranks held. They also yielded one other piece of information which was to direct my researches along a false trail. Both documents recorded that on leaving the Army he had been a member of the 18th (Pioneer) Battalion of the Middlesex Regiment.

Having exhausted the official documents available to me I turned to members of the family. There was a recollection that he had been gassed and wounded at least once, and probably twice, though not seriously enough for him to be returned to England. His sister recalled a vivid memory of the infested state of his uniform when he came home from France on leave, when it proved necessary for him to strip off his clothing and throw it out of the window to be dealt with later. She also recalled their mother carefully ironing the seams of his uniform in order to destroy the lice lurking there. Such anecdotal evidence was interesting but did not take me much further. However one document did come to light which was to provide the key to all my subsequent researches. Clement's sister had preserved a cutting from the journal of the Tilehouse Baptist Church dated January 1920 (The Norris family were all members of that Church). The cutting contained a report of the action during which Clement's had earned the award of the Military Medal and its detailed nature strongly suggested that it had been written with reference to the official citation. It read as follows:

"It is somewhat late in the day to congratulate our young friend Mr. Clement Norris, son of Mr and Mrs Fred Norris, on being awarded the Military Medal. With the modesty which normally obtains with those who do meritorious deeds it has been difficult to get particulars until now.

It was during the attack at Briastre, near Le Caute (sic), on the morning of October 12th 1918 our young friend was in charge of a Lewis gun[1] with which he did such good work that his conduct earned the distinction of 'conspicuous gallantry'. Subsequently the enemy counterattacked and owing to some weakness on the right and left flanks our forces were obliged to retire. During this retirement our friend and a comrade again proved their bravery by securing the gun and getting it into action and so covered the retreat and assisted our men in getting back.

Clement Norris has seen some hard fighting but does not talk about it for he is as modest as he is brave. We are glad to know his bravery has been appreciated."

This was a helpful and exciting piece of evidence for in addition to providing an account of the action it also gave me a precise date and two place names. However, a study of maps of

---

[1] The Lewis gun was an air-cooled, relatively lightweight gun with a 50-round rotary magazine. A 100-round magazine was available for aircraft use.

France and Belgium revealed no such place as "Le Caute" and it was some time before I realised that this must have been a typing error for Le Cateau. My supposition was confirmed when on a detailed Michelin map I found the small village of Briastre some eight kilometres north of Le Cateau.

I had now to look further afield - to the Imperial War Museum. Among the collection of regimental histories I found a mine of information: Wyrall's two volume history of the Middlesex Regiment "*The Die-hards in the Great War*", and with mounting excitement I searched for the activities of the 18th Battalion on 12th October 1918, only to be disappointed. It was clear that that particular battalion had not been in the vicinity of Le Cateau on that date. However the book did contain a detailed account corresponding in all particulars with the Church newspaper cutting of an engagement on 12th October, but the unit involved was the 4th Battalion of the Middlesex Regiment.

Confused, I returned to Hitchin and wrote to the Ministry of Defence (Army Medal Office) in Droitwich, hoping to obtain a copy of the Military Medial citation. I was informed that citations for Military Medals awarded in 1914-18 are no longer held, but I was sent an extract from the London Gazette Supplement dated 17th June 1919 which read as follows:

Middlesex Regiment
6670 Pte. Norris, C.,
4th Bn. (Hitchin)

Here then was the solution to my puzzle. Clearly Clement had served with the 4th Battalion in 1918, and perhaps before when it had been heavily engaged in the Battle of Arras in 1917, but after the Armistice he had presumably been transferred to the 18th Battalion. Probably the 4th had been disbanded early on, and it was likely that in the aftermath of war a Pioneer battalion like the 18th would have been retained in Belgium to assist in clearance and reconstruction.

I could now study Wyrall's account of the activities of the 4th Battalion with renewed interest, knowing that Clement had been a member. The Spring of 1918 saw the last great German offensive on the Western Front, but by the late summer the British army had repulsed the enemy and was able to go over to the attack. The 4th Battalion, as part of the 37th Division, advanced from Gommecourt via Bapaume to engage in the successful assault on the Hindenburg Line. By September the German army was falling back upon a hastily prepared defence line, named the Hermann Position, on the hills immediately to the east of the small river Selle - close to where one of the earliest battles of the war (Le Cateau) had been fought by the British Expeditionary Force in 1914. Although the Germans had not had sufficient time to dig an elaborate trench system they had erected extensive barbed wire defences. In addition the position possessed great natural strength. In the valley lay the river which had been dammed to give a depth of about six feet. Some distance up on the hillsides ran a railway, parallel to the river, with a series of embankments and cuttings which provided German infantry and particularly the machine gunners with excellent cover from which to sweep the valley. The slopes of the hillsides beyond gave artillery splendid opportunity for dominating the approaches to the river. As the German army was by now in danger of complete collapse its commanders regarded defence of the Hermann Position beside the Selle as of vital importance, and were determined to make a stand.

Such was the awesome task facing the 4th Middlesex as, in the van of the advance, they advanced down the western slopes of the Selle Valley on 11 October having fought all the way from Gommecourt. The orders for the following day were that they, together with a battalion of the New Zealand Division on their left and a Manchester battalion from the 17th Division on their right, were to advance in the early hours across the river and establish bridgeheads from which a subsequent general advance could be launched. The attack began with an artillery barrage which enabled the Middlesex to advance up the hill but which was less effective on the left in front of the New Zealanders. In particular the machine gunners in a group of farm buildings called Belle Vue alongside the railway line not only held the New Zealanders at bay but they also directed heavy enfilade fire on the left flank of the Middlesex such that the latter were forced to retire back down the hill. On the right flank also other British units were repulsed, hence the Middlesex were (as clearly described in the report in the church magazine) so endangered on both flanks that they were forced to retreat to the river in the valley. Thus Clement Norris and a fellow soldier made effective use of their Lewis gun to cover their comrades' retreat across the railway line and a parallel road, and back through the barbed wire defences. Such an action would have helped to save many lives, and this probably accounted for the award of the Military Medal. The Middlesex who now gathered near the river had suffered a reverse, but the Germans were not allowed to claim a final victory. The British soldiers were reinforced and in the early evening, at 6 p.m., they mounted a second attack which was completely successful. Even the stubborn defenders of Belle Vue were overcome and a bridgehead was established across the river. At this point the Middlesex withdrew from the fray having lost 22 killed, 101 wounded and 15 missing, but they had succeeded in their task for eight days later, on 20th October, other units began to move forward from the Selle bridgeheads and on to the Forest of Mormal and the Sambre River. It was to be an advance which would stop only on the declaration of the Armistice on 11th November.

General Ludendorff, the German commander on the Western Front, is reported as saying in early October that an orderly withdrawal of his armies was dependent on two basic requirements, namely that the Americans had to be held on the Argonne front and the British on the River Sale. In neither was he successful and his failure precipitated dismissal by the Kaiser on 26th October. The overwhelming victory of the Allied armies which followed in November 1918 was due to the heroism of countless individuals among whom was the kindly young baker from Hitchin, Lance-Corporal Clement Norris, M. M.

Brian Grant
Huddersfield, W. Yorks.

REFERENCES

This account of military operations on the Selle has used information drawn from a number of sources chief among which are the following:

Brook-Shepherd, G., *November 1918, The Last Act of the Great War*, Collins, 1981

Edmonds, J.E., and Hyslop, R. M., *Military Operations in France and Belgium 1918*, Vol.V, H.M.S.O., (London), 1947

Maurice, F. *The Last Four Months*, Cassell (London), 1919.

Wyrall, E. *The Die-Hards in the Great War*, Vol.II., Harrison (London) 1930.

Vol 9 no 4, December 1993

Where I Went to School in Hitchin

Derek Fosdike

Schools have always played a great part in the history of Hitchin, its present, and I'm sure its future. We hear of the British Schools, the Church of England schools, the Grammar Schools and the more common schools. I wonder how many younger people know of, or the older people remember the not so common schools.

When I arrived in Hitchin in 1944 with my mother and brother, I was eight years old. My brother was twelve, so in our schooling he was always four years in front of me. He never attended the primary but went straight into the senior schools.

My first school was nearly next door to where I lived in Queen Street. Not the British School, but next door to it.[1] My classroom was upstairs at the back of the Wesleyan Chapel. Because of the influx of evacuees the schools soon became overcrowded and children were taught wherever there was a space for a classroom. Our playground was the yard at the front and graves at the back. They were 'out of bounds' but we played on them anyway.

I seem to recall one teacher in particular from each school I attended. The teacher at the Wesleyan Chapel was Mrs Phillips (I think she was married to Mr Phillips the Geography teacher at Old Hale Way Boys' School, where I was to finish my schooling). The one thing which she taught me that I have never forgotten was how to make a Christmas decoration from an egg and a milk bottle top. Milk bottle tops in those days were made of cardboard

---

[1] Now demolished, replaced by Wilshere Court.

with a perforated ring in the middle, to enable you to push your finger in, and then hook the top out of the bottle.

Very often the perforations didn't go right through the cardboard, then you pressed hard and you and your nearest neighbour would get a milk shower. A piece of wool was tied around the matchstick then threaded through the milk top, then the egg shell and the paper cone, a spot of glue on each and a loop was made at the top to hook on to the tree. We made all our own decorations in those days, paper chains etc....

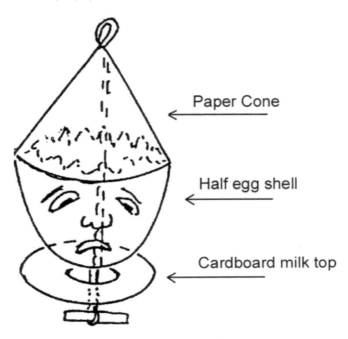

Right: Derek's drawing of the Christmas decoration, as taught to him by Mrs Phillips. The face doesn't look that cheerful for a Christmas decoration.

Paper Cone

Half egg shell

Cardboard milk top

I went to the same school as my brother for a little while, this was Grove House. It was a big white house on the corner of Grove Road and Cadwell Lane (actually a few yards into Cadwell Lane). It had a drive, or more like a yard, that led down from Cadwell Lane to the front of the house. There was a coal house (all part of the main building) on the left, which we would play in given half a chance. At the back, the grounds went right down to the woods and the river at Grove Mill. We played here also. This was out of bounds, as was the coal house, but it is always more fun playing where you shouldn't.

The teacher I remember here was Mr Cox, the Headmaster. He used to play the piano at assembly in the main hall. I expect it was a big room but to a little lad like me it was a hall. One morning while playing he struck several discords (not that us children noticed), which were bad enough to make him stop playing and investigate the back of the piano. After lifting the lid (it was an old upright) he soon discovered the cause. About six or eight of his canes had been hidden in there. He was very fond of wielding his cane. I don't remember him ever using it on a child but he used it to emphasise his speech by whacking the table or a chair with it. It was also good for gaining our attention. The big boys would watch out for when he left one laying around and would promptly hide it and it seemed that the piano was a favourite hiding place.

Above: The rear of Grove House, from approximately north. The building is now demolished. (North Hertfordshire Museum Service)

I went from Grove House to another 'church' school. This time it was the Baptist Church at the top of Tilehouse Street next to the Highlander Public House. As you go in through the front gate there is an annex to your right which housed our classrooms. Our playground was the yard at the front of the church. I recollect a few small trees which were struggling for life. The reason I remember them or rather one in particular was this:- A favourite game we boys played was Cavaliers or Musketeers. We would wear our raincoats/overcoats in cape fashion secured only by the top button around our necks, then ride our bikes at breakneck speed around the yard. I was riding mine (Look, mum, no hands, style) not watching where I was going, went under a low branch and in the best Hollywood tradition was knocked clean from the saddle. I have exercised greater care ever since.

The teacher, or head teacher as she would be known now, that I remember from Tilehouse Street school was Miss Colthard. I remember her from her car, a Jowett Saloon.[1] I can see it now, all shining black. It's not difficult to remember as I didn't know anybody else who owned a car in those days.

My next move was to the Sea Cadets Hut on the Bedford Road almost opposite what is now the Angels Reply Public House *[now renamed the Angel]*. Our play area was the parade

---

[1] Jowetts produced cars with alliterative names – the *Jupiter* and the *Javelin*, and some zoological ones – the *Blackbird*, the *Flying Fox* and the *Weasel*. The company was liquidated in 1954. I rather like the idea of a car called a Weasel... SLW.

ground, and around the 'clinker' built lifeboat that used to hang from davits just outside the hut. There were a lot of M. O. D. huts close to our hut where we used to chase the girls. 'Kiss Chase' was a favourite game at this particular edifice of education. Two girls that every boy tried to catch were Barbara and Zelda, and yes, I can also remember their surnames! It was an annex of Wilshere Dacre School. They had no room to house us, as I said before, not even for school dinners. At dinner time we would make our own way to the Old Town Hall where dinners were provided. After dinner, we would roam around the town. Being boys with an appetite, we would still be hungry and would sometimes buy a penny's worth of broken biscuits from Woolworths. If it was bad weather we would take a hushed walk around St Mary's Church which was always open. Other times we would go to Windmill Hill and dare each other to walk the length of the tunnel that went from the bottom of the hill under Walsworth Road to the top of Hermitage Road. We had no lights, only matches and I never did make it to the other end. Though was told at the end of the tunnel there was an iron studded door. I wonder where it led to![1]

My teacher at the Sea Cadets Hut (who, alas, not long ago went to teach at that big University in the sky) was Mr Boffin. I remember him well. He had a unique way of teaching. He would set us our work for the lesson and when he was satisfied we were getting down to it, he would then sit at the piano (I don't know what a piano was doing there) and play gentle classical music all through the lesson.

From the Sea Cadets Hut I 'graduated' to the big boys' school. Old Hale Way (boys). I know there is nothing uncommon about this school as with the other four, but I would like to include it as it was my last school. There was one teacher there that I must mention in order to make my story complete. The teacher that I remember, perhaps more than any other, and not without some affection, was Mr Burwell, the school's art teacher, known to all the boys (but not to his face) as 'Billy' Burwell. I had a little talent in the art field as did a classmate, Tony 'Bunny' Ashwell. From our first year I think Mr Burwell recognised this and encouraged us all he could. We longed for art periods to come round and in the meantime, we would spend lunch hours in the art room. If not engaged in actual art, then we would be in the store room tidying it up, cleaning out old jars of paint etc.

We lived for art and would bring in work done in our spare time to show each other and of course Mr Burwell, who would always give encouraging constructive criticism. I can't speak for 'Bunny' but I think it was through Mr Burwell's eyes that I was shown the beauty in other fields - furniture, music, clocks, nature and indeed life itself. I owe Mr Burwell a large debt of gratitude. In our last year (1951), we were asked if we would like to paint a mural on the wall

---

[1] Despite rumours that the tunnel under Walsworth road was built by monks, and ran to the Priory, the truth is more mundane: George Beaver, surveyor, recorded in his diary that 'on 18th February 1880] a plan for a subway from Mr. Seebohm's Hermitage Grounds to his Rawling's Dell and Windmill Hill Woods and Pleasure Grounds to pass under the Walsworth Road…'

at the foot of the main stairs. We painted a farmyard scene and started a trend. After our success, each year the best artists in their last year were invited to scrub off the previous year's effort and to replace it with their own.

I have never taken it up as a profession, never having had the opportunity, but I sketch and paint whenever I can, which is not as often as I'd like. Last year I entered the logo competition run by the Hitchin Historical Society and was fortunate enough to win, so looking back I suppose I owe that, in part, to Mr. 'Billy' Burwell.

Vol 10 no 1, May 1994

Tommy Chamberlain's Shop

Derek Else

I have reached an age when it may be of some interest to recall a few memories of what is now Hitchin's history. Not the large events but a few links with people and places. I thought of this when I saw in Hitchin Museum, among several old advertisements, one for Tommy Chamberlain, Baker and Confectioner etc.

T. Chamberlain, BAKER AND ❧ ❧ ❧ ❧ ❧ CONFECTIONER

Cakes for Teas, from 4d., 5d.
and 6d. per lb.
Good Dough Cakes, 3d. per lb.

WHEATMEAL BREAD A SPECIALITY.

T. C. attends Hitchin Market on Tuesdays, when all orders may be left at his Stall.

41, WHINBUSH ROAD, HITCHIN.   *PONY & TRAP LET ON HIRE.*

After the First World War I lived as a boy at 59 Whinbush Road, Hitchin, the house where I was born. My father and mother ran a laundry business, started by my father before the war, in premises behind the house. Built on the side of the house, with a through door from the kitchen, was a timber structure which we called "the shop". It had three large windows, one of them sliding (at what could have been the height of a counter) and another door opening on to the drive leading to stables close to the River Hiz. My father, who had lived at the house with his brother Tom before his marriage, told me that "the shop" had previously been kept by a baker named Tommy Chamberlain and it had various uses during my boyhood.

At times I used it as a playroom where, as I grew older, I appreciated the gaslight and gas point to which I could attach an ancient gas fire and sometimes a bunsen burner for my chemistry experiments (using my Christmas present). On a long shelf faced the sliding window (did it display loaves in Tommy Chamberlain's day?) I stored hundreds of Oxo coupons (does anyone recall collecting them?) which were eventually exchanged for my first cricket bat - a good one - not a toy. This was greatly prized. At that time to have your own cricket bat or perhaps better still your own football, made you a leader in the games played mainly on Ransom's Recreation Ground. The room was once occupied as a bed-sitter by newly married friends of my mother's. Reg was in the RAF at Henlow Camp and with little money to spare he would, when on night duty, place his cycle lamp battery by the kitchen fire to revive it, snatch it up and pedal off hoping to get to work before the lamp failed. "Riding without lights" (often mentioned in police court news) was a serious offence in those days!

In the old advertisement Tommy Chamberlain describes his business at No 41 (not 59) Whinbush Road. Referring to old trade directories I found that Chamberlain occupied premises in Whinbush Road at least from 1895 until 1914. In 1914 my father appears as "Laundry Proprietor". The number 41 appears until the 1906 directory changing to 59 in 1910, a small mystery which perhaps someone can explain.[1]

Postscript: I am told by an eye-witness that when the premises were demolished in 1962 they just collapsed in a cloud of dust, lathes and plaster! Now we have Kennedy Court!

Vol 10 no 1, May 1994

Hitchin in the Late 1920s to Late 1940s

Marshall F Dellar

My earliest memories are of the old British School in Queen Street. No school buses in those days and no school dinners. I believe we did get a third of a pint of milk in a small bottle and a straw to drink it with. We had hard wooden benches to sit on and wooden type of desks with a slate and a thing I believe was called a "scriber," later replaced with pencils and paper. Dinner was from 12.00 until 2.00pm and lessons finished about 4 o'clock. The toilets were situated at the top end of the playground and were they cold in winter! One did not hang around too long!

Hitchin was quite a bustling small town. In the late 1930's it had one cinema called "The Playhouse" where silent films were shown accompanied by someone on a piano. We also had a theatre in the town called Blakes in Ickleford Road. The original building is still there just on the right by the Post Office and News shop. Some good shows were put on there, even mini circuses with trapeze and tightrope artistes in attendance.

---

[1] As the town developed, some streets were renumbered. Normal practice was for odd numbers to be on one side of the road and even numbers on the other. If however development was such that only one side was developed, the houses still needed numbers. What do you do if the other side is developed later on? The answer was sometimes to renumber the whole road.

Above: Hitchin British School, Queen Street. From the rear.   The 1857 school building is on the right. Houses for the Master and Mistress to the left. (Wikipedia, public domain).

Going back to the Playhouse we used to pay two pence in old money for admission, about one penny in our money today. As we went in the torches which we tried to smuggle in were taken from us and returned at the end of the film show! Many a torch was claimed by some other boy if it was better than the one he had in the first place. The retained half of the admission ticket was carefully guarded until the interval when a free draw was made, often for a clockwork train set (a luxury in those days), lead soldiers and a mini fort, large dolls for girls and boxes of sweets and chocolates. We used to queue up to get in and next to the passageway belonging to Hobley's where cakes and doughnuts were being made. The smells were wonderful; I'm sure all of us had mouths watering and nostrils all of a quiver.

A word or two about the market held in the square that still bears the same name now remodelled but not particularly liked by a lot of elder residents of the town. All the stalls were lit in those days by hissing paraffin lamps that had to be kept pumped up to keep them alight and bright. They had mantles which gave quite a good light and a certain amount of warmth.

One stall that stood opposite to the Rose & Crown and sticks in my mind was "Garratt and Cannons." You've guessed it - a sweet stall, all home made by a family run factory in Hitchin.

For a penny we could buy a lucky bag chocked full of goodies, mis-shaped sweets, toffees with the odd chocolate, a locust bean and chewy meringue type of sweet.

Right: the Playhouse Theatre was to the right of the Corn Exchange in the Market Place. (Simon Walker)

One day in a very strong wind the stall blew over but unfortunately I was not one of the boys nearby. I was told afterward that there was one mad rush and in a very few minutes every sweet had been picked up from the ground! There must have been some very sticky pockets about after that!

Another stall was the toffee and rock man. What a lovely smell of fruit and peppermint and boiling sugar! When it was cooked he would pour it onto a large board to cool awhile. When it was warm and soft he would throw it over a large hook suspended on high and pull and stretch it repeatedly until it had cooled sufficiently to be made into chunks or put through a small machine and made into small sweets ready to be sold to the waiting public.

Yet another stall that stood in the centre of the market was known as "Cheap Jack's". It was run by two Jewish gentlemen from London who used to come on the train with two or three suit cases rammed full of goodies. Ingersoll wrist or pocket watches could be bought for half-a-crown along with playing cards, scissors, combs, pocket knives and things too numerous to mention. They would be transported to and from the station by Boxall's taxis even up to a few years ago and must have traded for 60 to 70 years.

Shops around the town centre included Spurr's Haberdashery & Ladies Clothes, Gatward's the jewellers and Allingham's Butchers, the latter two still trading today. Then there was the

British Legion tea rooms, Melias, Timothy Whites the ironmongers and chemist and two other grocers shops.

In Sun Street you had Morris's the bakers, and Crees the wet fish shop with live lobsters on the marble slabs moving their feelers so you could tell that they were fresh. Also the music shop Rollason's – a good place to buy a harmonica - and Morgan's the motor cycle shop, the only one to survive. Now into Bridge Street - Parker's Fruit & Veg; up the yard the blacksmiths & workshop, the little sweet shop next to Parker's where you had to duck your head to get through the door. Then there was Bottoms Hill View Restaurant, Lewin's sweet shop and cafe and not least Holland's Fish & Chip shop. Going on to Bucklersbury there was Hawkins the Clothiers. Next door was the pawn shop run by Mr Morley. The bracket where the three brass balls used to hang from can still be seen today over the door. Also don't let me forget Squire's Dairies where the best ice cream in town could be purchased.

Hitchin was not a bad place to live in those days with always something going on. The fairs at Butts Close still come to Hitchin today. I wonder how many folk can remember a fair held about sixty years or more ago behind the Three Moorhens public house at the top of Hitchin Hill. Last but not least we had Sir Alan Cobham[1] and his air display team on Buryfield with all the fun of the fair with side stalls and shows and the man diving off a hundred foot tower into a small round tank of water. He was set alight before he jumped. For those who do not remember Buryfield it is where Strathmore Avenue, Old Hale Way and Heathfield Road now stand.

One other memory was when they built St. Mary's Square and the ornamental river. Near the Biggin, a great landmark to the town; the water was clean in those days, so fresh from the springs at Wellhead and Charlton that the children used to swim therein. Another favourite watering place was at Cadwell; we used to call it Sandy Bottom. There was also the old Hitchin swimming pool in Queen Street, still there as a static water tank I believe.[2] Didn't it used to be cold at the beginning of the summer season, the water was not heated in those days - Brrrrr!

Sunday was a special day for us children. We had to dress in our best clothes and go to Sunday School and later if the weather was kind we would be taken for a long walk with our parents. One of my favourite walks was over Priory Park to Charlton then on to the ford near Wellhead and up the lane to Gosmore, to pause for a while at one of the pubs in the village. There used to be three at that time and if we had been of good behaviour we would maybe get a glass of lemonade and a large penny "arrowroot biscuit". I remember them as almost the size of a saucepan lid.

---

[1] See *Hitchin: Glimpses of the Past*, pp 76-83 for a detailed account of Sir Alan Cobham's visit to Hitchin.
[2] Queen Street swimming baths are no more; the site is now given over to housing.

One other road that was of interest was Nightingale Road, home of the Bacon Factory. What aromas used to emanate from there, some pleasant and some not so! There was also the Doll's Hospital where you could take any broken doll to be repaired for a small charge. Also there was "Aunties" sweet shop next door to Mrs Williams' Corset Shop. Opposite was the British Red Cross house where the nurse used to give electric massage treatment to broken bones etc.

NIGHTINGALE ROAD, HITCHIN. NO. 18.

Above: Nightingale Road c. 1920. The Bacon Factory is the range of buildings on the right. (SLW)

There was the Gas Works at Starlings Bridge, Furr's Fish Shop and Johnnie Howard's Fruit & Veg shop. I wonder how many people remember Ruby who served in shop and how many thought she was Johnnie's wife – but she was not! Of course I must not forget to mention Tilehouse Street with one of the oldest firms in Hitchin, Francis Newton. It is not commonly known that the original F Newton was a direct relative of Sir Isaac Newton.[1] Then there was the old tithe barn at the rear of Shadbolt's which was used as the Hitchin Boys' Club. I have many happy memories – Mr Day the basket maker sitting outside the house weaving baskets

---

[1] We have found no evidence that the Newtons were direct descendants of Sir Isaac Newton. Reginald Hine in his History of Hitchin Vol II pp391-392 talks about Isaac Newton of the Hitchin Fire Brigade being 'given the name of the illustrious Sir Isaac, the pride of their family.' It seems likely that, had Hine any direct evidence, he would have mentioned it. Sir Isaac Newton never married, and is not known to have fathered any children out of wedlock.

out of cane and reeds, Lamb's sweet shop, Foster's carpenters shop, Cooper the butchers and at the top Hidgecock the bakers, one of three baker's brothers in Hitchin.

GEORGE DAY,

Basket Maker, Cane, Wicker and Rush Worker.

●●●●●●▲●●●●●●●●●●●●●●●●●●●

English and Foreign Baskets in Stock and to Order.
ORDERS RECEIVE PERSONAL ATTENTION.

●●●●●▲●●●●●▲●●●●●●●●●●●●●

12, TILEHOUSE STREET, HITCHIN.

Above: this advertisement for George Day, basket maker, appeared in 1920 (SLW)

The pubs in Hitchin in the thirties were very numerous. About thirty two were in the vicinity of the town centre. Beer was 4d a pint and cigarettes were five for 2d. If one had a florin (10p) in those days a good night on the tiles could be had! Things were not too bad in the thirties as long as one had employment; the wages were low but so were the prices.

In those days tradesmen were seen around the town hawking their wares; the milkman with his horse and cart with two large churns from which he would ladle out pint or half pint measures of milk and pour into the jugs brought out by the womenfolk; the sarsaparilla man who sold some sort of herbal concoction; the muffin man ringing his bell dispensing muffins and crumpets and the coalman with brands of best household coal - "London Cobbles" and "Derby Brights" are two of the brands I still remember costing about one shilling to one and sixpence a hundredweight.

One other vivid memory of those days was the crystal sets we used to make. If you were lucky you had a set with one valve and a pair of ear-phones. Later on battery powered radio sets came along which had a large 9v battery, an accumulator and a smaller screen grid. I used to return home from school and there would be my father working at the kitchen table with a soldering iron and a blueprint busy making radios. He used to cut intricate patterns in the cabinet with a fret saw. Some people used to swear he was the best radio man in Hitchin, anyone who had a fault with their radio Dad would find it.

Houses were lit by gas light and I remember the lamp-lighter used to ride around on his bike and light the street lamps with a taper on a long stick; sometimes he would climb up the lamp and fit new mantles in them.

One day I shall never forget was when Woolworth's store first came to Hitchin.[1] They were called the "Threepence and Sixpence" stores. In America, from whence they originated, they were called the "Nickel and Dime" store. Our Christmas presents were purchased from there and much appreciated. I don't know what today's children would think of that but times change, not I may add always for the better.

My wrist begins to ache, I hope this little narrative will be of interest to members of the Historical Society.

Vol 10 no 2, August 1994

A Victorian Cottage in Hitchin

Chris and Trina Hubbard

[Note: Chris and Trina no longer live in the cottage. SLW]

Some of you may have already visited our cottage in St John's Road, either in the winter or the summer and so will be familiar with its contents and surroundings. However for those who haven't yet managed it, I shall presently detail some of the items you could see and would also have been likely to see in a cottage of the period.

Firstly though perhaps you would like to know a little of the background to the row of thirteen cottages. They were built in 1898 by a Mr John James and were named Providence Terrace, and accordingly there is an in-built stone plaque over number 31. I know this, as I picked out the words and date in black paint myself. An old chap, now sadly deceased, used to recall that his father helped to build the cottages and that they were built for £90.00 each. The bricks were apparently made at the small brickfield where the playing fields in the road now stand. At the time of building the road was called Bethel Lane and was changed to St John's Road between 1926/28, probably after the chapel of that name, which itself had formerly been known as Bethel Chapel up to the 1870s or 1880s.

Now to return to the cottage itself. My wife Trina and I have tried to make it look representative in that the contents generally date from about the 1880's through to the First World War. The first room you would have stepped into would have been, of course, the Front Room or Parlour as it was more widely termed. It was a room hardly used and was reserved for Sundays and visitors. Because of this, a coal fire was lit only when necessary and therefore it tended to be pretty cold in the winter months. Since it was not a regularly used living room, most of the nice pieces, those that the family possessed, were housed there. In ours you have the mahogany veneered china display cabinet, and separately the

---

[1] This building now houses Boots Chemist.

chiffonier. I remember my dear gran had a chiffonier, and a harmonium, which was put to use every Sunday evening for the accompaniment of Wesleyan Hymns when my father, now 87, was a boy. I had a chance of buying one just recently but lack of space unfortunately dictated otherwise.

Our display cabinet is used to the full and houses a Victorian tea service, posy holders in various guises of little boys and girls, made of porcelain and probably imported from Germany, as were a lot of the knick-knacks and seaside ware at that time. Things haven't changed much have they?

Above: The Living Room, or Parlour, in Providence Terrace. (Chris and Trina Hubbard)

As further entertainment we have a wind up gramaphone with a splendid brass horn plus the requisite old records, and pretty awful they sound too. For furniture we have a lovely old Victorian sofa, a couple of balloon - back side chairs, a rush seated arts and crafts style chair and a small nursery chair.

The walls are covered with old family photos and prints, mostly of a religious theme, and seaside ware. "Shell Pictures" is one of a seaside scene and another is of the then Prince and Princess of Wales. There is plenty of evidence of chintz, lace and chenille (as there is throughout the whole house) all favoured soft furnishing materials. The room though is dominated by a lovely tiled cast iron fireplace with a Victorian beaded surround, topped off by an over-mantle mirror. The mantelpiece has a French black slate clock on either side of which is a pair of Staffordshire flat back figures. We have cheated by having central heating but when the coal fires in both living rooms are on the go this is quite superfluous! Incidentally our modern slim-line radiators are soon to be replaced by ornate Victorian-style cast iron ones!

The " Living Room" (which is also used as our dining room) was used as the name suggests and must have been very claustrophobic, bearing in mind that the family on average would comprise Mum, Dad and possibly four or even likely more children. I have to say straight away that we have really gone over the top in comparison to what you actually would have seen in a "working man's" cottage, but everything is representative of the range of items you might have seen. Having said that, clutter and lots of it, was certainly the order of the day, but this more likely occurred in a middle class household. Again the centre piece of the room is the fireplace, cast iron and tiled but this time with a pine surround which is laden with Staffordshire dogs and figures and a watchholder.

Above: The Bedroom, and below, the bathroom. (Chris and Trina Hubbard)

Virtually all of one side of the room is taken up by a splendid Lincolnshire pine dresser, and so much stuff is on there that it's difficult to see the wood for the china! It especially houses my Gran's lovely tea service, a wedding present when she and Grandad were married in July 1901. They came up this way from Kent in 1914. Gran's sister, my Aunt Liza, was married to Augustus "Gus" Orsman and they lived all their married lives in that lovely old house in

Bedford Road named "Kenwood". They had two sons, my Uncles Percy, (the black sheep of the family) and Bertram, who was a highly competent organist and played at St Mary's and Brand Street Wesleyan. Grandad worked as a gardener for W B Moss and he and Gran lived in Bedford Street, where Gus owned the corner shop, and quite a few houses in the road. My father went to the British School until he was fifteen and is probably one of the oldest "old boys" left. He remembered - and sang - the School song when Brian Limbrick recently taped his memories.

Above: The bathroom. (Chris and Trina Hubbard)

Sorry I've digressed a bit, so back to the dresser and its contents. Other than Gran's tea service there are numerous jugs, bread plates, cheese dishes, teapots, jelly moulds and other kitchenalia. We eat on a lovely old pine farmhouse table which is covered by a highly decorative chenille tablecloth, and when not in use, we have a bird's nest and asparagus fern in rose decorated jardinières. Around the walls are plenty of commemorative plates, plaques, family photos and prints.

There are two bedrooms and I'll detail one of these only, that is, the main bedroom. The general theme regards decoration and objects is roses, so one is reminded of Summer days throughout the whole year. The draped four-poster bed is in the centre of the room and the walls have framed religious mottos, samplers and photos. There are two washstands, two pine dressers and five sets of jugs and bowls! It's not that we're personal hygiene fanatics, it's just that we can't resist a rose printed jug. Rather than wall to wall carpeting the floor boards have been painted black, with rugs thrown down.

The bathroom has just recently been completely re-styled to match a Victorian setting. A roll-top cast iron bath, high level WC and period style wash basin have been installed. The general decor follows suit with pine panelling topped off by a dado rail and old style skirting boarding really creates the right atmosphere. A touch of greenery is supplied by a tall Areca palm in an old jardinière, set on a bamboo plant stand.

We've tried to maintain authenticity with the lighting and brass taps and accessories. We're really pleased with the end result and hope our visitors enjoy it as much as we do - in fact we hope they enjoy everything they see as much as we do.

Vol 10 no 2, August 1994

Past into Present: Hitchin's Old Dispensary

David Howlett

When the new Safeway supermarket *[now Waitrose – SLW]* was constructed on the Lairage the adjacent building which formed the original core of the Hitchin Infirmary - now known as Thomas Bellamy House after its architect – was refurbished. Unfortunately, despite the fact that the Infirmary itself is an important listed building, the adjoining "Old Dispensary" was allowed to deteriorate into an eyesore which now mars the whole site.

The label "Old Dispensary" draws attention to the Infirmary's links with a charitable dispensary that was founded at No 14 High Street in 1823 by Dr Frederick Hawkins for the needs of the town's sick poor. This Hitchin example reflected a national movement that had developed from the 1770's designed to provide health care for the poor in the most cost effective way possible as befitted an activity wholly reliant on charitable donations. Ordinary houses and cottages could be adapted for dispensary work (hence the original location in High Street) and purpose built accommodation normally had to wait until the institution was firmly grounded in local support. When the Hitchin Infirmary was established in 1840 the new hospital subsumed the functions of the High Street Dispensary.

As the nineteenth century wore on greater attention was given to the provision of specialised buildings for specialised medical functions. For example *The Builder* of 1849 contained an account of the new Eastern Dispensary in Bath, describing it as "a suggestive type." The Eastern Dispensary was of a square plan with a central top-lit dispensing room surrounded by circulation passages. A main front entrance gave access to either surgeons' or physicians' waiting rooms, which had benches to seat patients in order of arrival, and then separate exits from the two consulting rooms via internal prescription windows where medicines were issued.

Research suggests that the present "Old Dispensary" in Hitchin began life in 1900 - 01 as a similar sort of "Outpatients Hall". A newspaper paragraph in the Lawson Thompson Scrapbooks (Vol 2B p237) notes that:

> "The Wing for the reception of Out Patients, nearly finished at the time of the last Annual Meeting was shortly afterwards completed.... The cost of this, including the Architects Commission, amounted to £2,524 5s 10d. Towards this sum subscriptions amounting to £2,383 3s 6d were acknowledged in the last report...
>
> "The new building for the reception of outpatients is now completed and will be of very great advantage to the Hospital. The cost of this and of alterations to the house in order to provide better accommodation for the staff will be about £2,500. Towards this amount about £2,400 has already been received or promised including a subscription of £1000 from Mr William Ransom."

The Hospital.   Hitchin.
209

Above: Hitchin Infirmary, from a contemporary postcard, c. 1920? The Outpatients' Department is on the left. [Jim Bowskill]

A current planning application for the Old Dispensary may well lead to its demolition. The site is certainly in need of major refurbishment given its linking position between Thomas Bellamy House and the Town Centre Conservation Area. It would be a great shame, however, if the Old Dispensary itself was totally swept away because, although it is not a Listed Building, it does provide a physical link with a group of local benefactors who worked hard to better the lives of many of their less fortunate townsfolk.

If any member is interested in investigating the story of the Hitchin Infirmary more can be discovered from Tony Foster's *Market Town* (1987) and Helen Poole and Alan Fleck's *Old Hitchin* (1978). The Museum has a collection of interesting material relating to the hospital and, as noted above, more general sources such as the Lawson Thompson Scrapbooks, include references to it. The Hertfordshire County Record Office (now Hertfordshire Archives and Local Studies) also has some archival material of relevance. Another volume worth consulting to place Hitchin developments more firmly in a national context is Jeremy Taylor's *Hospital and Asylum Architecture in England 1840 – 1914* (London 1991).

David Howlett

Vol 25 no 1, Spring 2015

It seems sensible to add the following document from North Hertfordshire Museum Service's archive:

Hitchin Dispensary,

March 29th, 1824.

AT the First General Meeting of the Governors and Subscribers, the Treasurer presented the subjoined account of the Donations and Subscriptions, and the expences attending the Establishment.

DR. F. HAWKINS delivered a report of the Patients admitted, and of the result of each case ; from which it appears that since the opening of the Institution, on the 19th day of October last, the number admitted has been FIFTY- TWO, of whom THIRTY-FOUR have been discharged cured, THREE relieved, TWO have died, and THIRTEEN now remain : he also reported, that many more had applied for admission, but owing to the present limited number of Subscribers, they could not obtain recommendations.

It is gratifying to the Meeting to find, that the Institution has, in its infancy, been the means of affording relief to so many sick persons, who might otherwise have been destitute ; and a confidence is entertained, that when the importance of the establishment, as a means of relief and comfort to the poor, shall be better known, there will be found such an increase of Benefactors, as considerably to extend the usefulness of the Institution.

The Subscribers present their sincere thanks to DR. HAWKINS for his benevolent and assiduous attention to the objects of the Charity.

The Subscribers will be happy to receive the assistance of the other Medical Practitioners in Hitchin.

Resolved, that the Annual Meetings of the Governors and Subscribers, be held on the last Monday of September.

W. WILSHERE, Chairman.

The Annual Subscriptions, which become due at Michaelmas, may be paid to Mr JOHN HAWKINS, the Treasurer, or at either of the Hitchin Banks.

The Treasurer's Account.

RECEIPTS	Donations.			Annual Subscriptions.				PAYMENTS.	£	s.	d.
	£	s.	d.	£	s.	d.	1823.	E. Perks for Medicines,	16	4	3
1823. Marquis of Salisbury,	10	10	0					Ditto in repayment for bottles,	5	4	4
Lord Dacre,	5	5	0					Ditto for drawers,	5	12	8
Hon. W. Lamb,	10	10	0					W. Langford for mahogany board,	1	4	0
Mr. Radcliffe,	10	10	0	2	2	0		J. Reynolds for painting,	1	5	0
Mr. Wilshere,	10	10	0	2	2	0		T. Paternoster for printing,	5	0	6
Mr. Heathcote,	10	10	0					J. Wilshere for coals,	0	3	3
Mr. Lautour,	5	5	0					E. Moore for advertisements,	0	8	7
Rev. H. Wiles,	3	3	0	2	2	0		P. Allen, Carpenter,	2	16	8
Rev. W. Lax,				1	1	0		J. Morgan, Stationer,	0	8	10
Rev. L. Burroughs,	2	2	0	1	1	0		J. Marks, Carpenter,	2	14	7
Rev. W. Pym,				1	1	0		G. Beaver for easy chairs,	2	14	0
Rev. W. W. Pym,				1	1	0		J. Paternoster for lining the same,	2	11	9
Mr. Eade,	3	3	0	2	2	0		Deposited in the Savings' Bank,	40	0	0
Mr. Ellis,				1	1	0		Balance,	8	12	1
Mr. Crabb,				2	2	0					
Mr. J. Hawkins,	2	2	0	2	2	0					
Mrs. Hawkins,				1	1	0					
Miss Hawkins,				0	10	6					
Mr. Bristow,				1	1	0					
Mr. Curling,				1	1	0					
	73	10	0	21	10	6					
				73	10	0					
				£95	0	6			£95	0	6

Paternoster, Printer, Hitchin.

In 1823 a voluntary dispensary was established at 14 Cock St, now High St, Hitchin, to look after the sick and lame poor in the town and vicinity. It was administered by a committee of governors and subscribers. The dispensary dealt only with patients recommended by the governors and subscribers. A medical officer gave his services free for two hours a week, and the hours were from 9am – 10am on Tuesdays and Saturdays. Patients in the town who were too sick to be moved, could be visited by the dispensary doctor. The overseers of the poor in Hitchin parish and neighbouring parishes were entitled to recommend patients according to the amount of their annual subscription. By 1829 thirty-one parishes were using the establishment and in that year 388 patients were treated. In those six years, the average cost was 4s (20p) per head. The subscribers felt the objects of the dispensary attained, but this alone could not deal with the more serious cases. In 1829 they established a fund from which grew the North Herts and South Beds Hospital. By 1840 Hitchin Infirmary was erected in Pound Lane, now Brand Street. It opened in October 1840, but the accommodation was insufficient. The governors were unwilling to increase it until they had cleared their debts of some £450 (this was achieved by 1844).

The number of beds was increased to twelve. Applications for admission increased. By the 1860s Hitchin doctors were performing operations under anaesthetic. By the late 1890s many of the parishes had a trained district nurse, but the number of patients still increased, mainly because of population growth. The hospital continued to be used mainly for the relief of the sick poor. Around 1900 the name changed to the North Hertfordshire and South Bedfordshire Hospital, reflecting the expanded origins of its clientele.

In 1948 the hospital became part of the NHS. The North Hertfordshire Maternity Unit at the same address continued separately up to 1982, but had moved to the new Lister Hospital in Stevenage by 1985.

The dispensary should not be confused with the Lister Hospital, off Maxwell Lane, which included wooden barrack wards built for Second World War wounded, and Hitchin Workhouse. The barracks closed in the early 1970s, though the remainder carried on as Hitchin Hospital, catering for geriatric patients, with parts still in use up to 2011.

Simon Walker

Vol 10 no 3, October 1995

Hitchin: A Post War Recollection of the Post Office
Marshall F Dellar

March 16th 1946, at last the great day had arrived! I was on my way home from *HMS Royal Katherine*, an ex-German U boat crews' rest camp situated at Buxtehude about sixteen miles from Hamburg.[1] I left Buxtehude by rail to Cuxhaven to embark on a ship bound for Hull, Yorkshire and then by train down to Chatham and demob from HM Forces; at last I arrived in *HMS Pembroke* in Chatham, Kent, then one of the three main naval bases in the UK (the others being Portsmouth and Plymouth).

My service life had consisted of three months training in *HMS Ganges* and two or three months at sea on *HMS Sheffield* (a town class cruiser), three months training for submarines and a course in sub-detection, now known as "Sonar". Then I was in service in submarines from 1942 to the summer of 1945 serving in the North and South Atlantic and a short time in the Mediterranean. After demob I joined the Royal Naval Volunteer Reserve, later transferred to the Royal Naval Reserve, until my fifty-fifth birthday.

On arrival in Chatham after doing joining routine (checking in etc.) it was off through the tunnel, a subterranean passageway built in a high cliff and used as air raid shelters, to the demobilisation centre in Victoria Barracks where we were fed and watered. Then those magic words over the tannoy: "Able Seaman Dellar..." I reported to the Regulating Office and thence went to the demob centre to be kitted out with civilian clothes; shirts, socks, shoes, suit (Harris Tweed), and, last but not least, a coat and hat (trilby). I wondered what my wife would think of me as a civvy, she had never seen me out of uniform!

We were put on a bus to Chatham railway station and transported home to Hitchin. My first priority was to find myself some sort of employment. I applied for work on the railway and was employed at the stock-yard adjacent to Benslow Bridge where we were kept hard at it making up new tracks and sleepers to replace the old tracks, badly worn and neglected due to the war years and the more pressing need for steel.

Right: Benslow Bridge, demolished with explosives early in the morning of Sunday, 27 July 1974 (Terry Wilson)

---

[1] HMS *Royal Katherine* produced a magazine called The Pied Piper between September 1945 and March 1946, when it ceased production. The Imperial War Museum has some copies https://www.iwm.org.uk/collections/item/object/1506000227 retrieved 9 March 2019.

Although I started work almost immediately, technically I was still in the Forces as I was on paid leave for several weeks after demobilisation. Forces pay in those days was only a pittance so it was imperative to get a job.

After working on the railway for a month or two I was offered a job with the Post Office being an ex-service man. So, on October 7 1946, I started working at the sorting office in Kings Road as a postman. I had to report to Inspector Geoff Cannon, a formidable man with a sergeant major's voice. It was five o'clock on a Monday morning. After signing the attendance sheet I was allocated to a postman on a walk who would instruct me how to "throw the letters off', an expression that means to place letters into partitions on a sorting frame of forty-eight partitions or boxes. Each box would be a street or part thereof. For example a large road or street would be broken down into several boxes and any large firm or business would have a box to themselves. After all the letters had been "thrown off" they had to be set in rotation according to the route on which they were to be delivered. They were also set in numerical order, tied up in bundles, and packed carefully in a pouch in the order of delivery. By this time it would be about seven o'clock and a start was made on the delivery round.

A memory that has stuck in my mind when on early morning delivery was the smell of people cooking bacon and eggs, especially on a cold and frosty morning. It was one of the nicest smells and made my mouth water! It's the same as when somebody passes you eating chips out of a bag.

In those days there were two or three deliveries of mail: two in the morning and one in the afternoon in town, but only two rural deliveries, morning and afternoon. Rain or shine they had to be done. It was often very difficult to keep letters dry, the pouches we carried them in used to get soaked. After delivery was completed it was back to the sorting office with the letters collected from the various pillar and post boxes situated on the route. There were also small packets and large envelopes from the sub-post offices dotted around the town, alas a lot of which are now closed. On reaching the sorting office the letters were segregated into separate bundles, long and short, ready to be put through the franking machine which would date and postmark them. After this it was time for breakfast which was by now more than welcome. We were allowed thirty minutes to eat our sandwiches; no canteen was available in those days although we did have a cup of tea which we made ourselves. There was a small kitchen where a quick fry-up could be made but it was not used very often in later years. We did eventually have a small canteen where a Mrs Colebrook would make us cheese, butter or fried bacon rolls at a reasonable price.

After breakfast it was back to the sorting frame where the town mail was "thrown off" into walks and the rurals into their own boxes. After the completion of sorting the procedure for delivery was repeated all over again.

There were various duties in the sorting office where the letters and packets and parcels had to be sorted into various categories such as primary sorting and then secondary sorting. After a certain time had elapsed it was time to tie all the letters into bundles and labelled for onward transmission to wherever they were going. These were placed in mail sacks and despatched by rail to London or Peterborough and thence all over the country.

Another job that I used to do was to despatch and collect mail by the "TPO" - Travelling Post Office. I did this job for several years. The mail bags would be placed in thick heavy pouches made of leather alongside the railway line. At a given sign from the railway signal box, a minute or so before the train was due, the arms of the apparatus holding the pouches would be turned towards the railway track and a large net was opened, also towards the track. This was to collect mail from the train, a wonderful two-way service.

Above: the interior of a TPO. (Thomas Nugent / Travelling Post Office interior / CC BY-SA 2.0)

A letter posted in the main post office in Hitchin at up to 8pm destined for Edinburgh would be delivered by 9am the next morning. The advent of the faster diesel trains gave the death knell to the TPOs as such on the lineside. The trains were too fast and the metal arms the bags were suspended from were being snapped off almost weekly. TPOs are still running but the special mail trains have to stop at certain rail stations, of which Hitchin is one, where vans from several locations gather and forward the bags of mail to the towns for which they are destined.[1]

My first winter with the PO was now approaching and I experienced my first Christmas. It was a real "eye opener" with all the extra staff it entailed and temporary men and women sorting all through the night the mountains of letters and packets. Parcels were sorted at a different location from letters, usually at the Drill Hall in Bedford Road, and letters at the Town Hall. After sorting was completed, or a cut off time was called, the mail was bundled and prepared for the temporaries to deliver. Two temps per round were allocated. On Christmas morning there was a slight change to routine; one half of the walk or round was delivered by the temp and the other half by the regular postman. After completion it was home to our families, by about 10am if we were lucky, with the rest of the day and Boxing Day off, then back to work to start all over again.

1947 arrived and what a winter it turned out to be! It seemed the worst winter ever and some of you reading this will remember seven weeks of ice, snow and hard frosts.

Left: Bancroft in the snow. 1947 was a hard winter, but 1962-3 (when this photograph was taken) was even worse, the coldest winter on record up to that year. But if anything the impact of the 1947 winter was greater, coming so soon after the Second World War. There were power cuts, and following the thaw there was extensive flooding. [SLW]

On level ground the snow was between one and a half and two feet deep. Streets such as Strathmore, Bearton and Lancaster Road and The Avenue were rutted with ice many inches

---

[1] Royal Mail decided to suspend all transportation of mail by rail in 2003 due to rising costs. The last TPO services went out on the night of 9 January 2004.

thick tempered by the slight thaw during the day then hard frost again at night. This went on for weeks making walking very difficult. I certainly had a good christening on my first winter.

One of the duties I recall was parcel delivery on a tricycle. This was a large basket on two wheels and a wheel and saddle at the back to sit on. The Inspector asked me if I could ride a trike and of course I said yes but, oh didn't I find out the hard way how difficult the trikes were to handle, with minds of their own like a modem supermarket trolley. I loaded up with parcels and started to pedal out of the yard into Kings Road then I turned into Nightingale Road but the trike wanted to go one way on its own and I wanted to go another. Up went one wheel in the air, the parcels were thrown out all over the road and the trike landed up on its side and I finished up on the road. After repacking the trike I carefully proceeded on my delivery with no further mishaps. I assumed I had conquered the brute but alas no; the braking arrangements were as follows: a lever on the handle of the basket worked the brake on the front wheels, another lever in front of the saddle worked the brake on the back wheel. It was not very successful, and if the front brake was applied too hard it would make the back lift up.

I must mention one incident which happened to me. I had been delivering in the upper Highbury area and was on my way back down Hollow Lane. Yes, you've guessed it - the brakes weren't powerful enough on the hill and I dared not take my hands off the handle bar. Faster and faster I careered down the hill but the Lord was watching over me. At the bottom of the hill it levels off and I was able to slow down and eventually stop the thing. Lucky in those days there wasn't that much traffic about. Phew! My hair has been grey ever since.

After a few months as a postman I was asked to take up driving duties so a trip to Hertford County Hall to renew my driving licence. A couple of day's tuition or refresher driver training was required. I soon started rural deliveries with my own mail van. My "rural" was Offley round in the morning and Gosmore, Preston, Kings Walden and Offley again in the afternoons. It was a lovely feeling being my own boss and meeting people on the rounds. Other rural rounds I learnt to deliver were Stotfold, Codicote, Kimpton and lastly Holwell and Ickleford. I have still got fond memories of some of the market gardeners and farmers I delivered to and often receiving a gift of a few eggs or a rabbit and even the occasional pheasant during the shooting season and also sprouts and cabbages and of course cups of tea.

I had several memorable events during my Post Office service. One very frosty morning whilst delivering in The Avenue in Hitchin I came across an elderly lady wandering about the road dressed only in a thin satin nightdress and bare feet. How she was not frost bitten I'll never know. Anyway I wrapped my overcoat round her and knocked on the nearest door and they took her in and called for medical help. Another episode also concerned another elderly lady, a Miss Woodcock in Stotfold. I had a registered letter to deliver to her and could not get an answer. Something made me look in the window and there she was lying on the floor. I tried the door and it was unlocked so I let myself in and managed with difficulty to lift her onto the bed.

She was very disoriented and as I knew the lady who cleaned for her I went straight to her house. Luckily she was in and she immediately called the doctor who came at once. He told me afterwards that I undoubtedly saved her life. If she had been left much longer she would not have survived.

One further incident is worthy of mention. I rang the bell of a cottage one morning and a young and quite attractive young woman opened the door. To my astonishment she was completely naked! How I managed to keep calm never know but having been warned by another postman about the said person being a bit odd I handed the package over and made a quick exit to the mail van.

Work at the Post Office was not easy. I was regularly up at 4.30am and cycled to the office to start work at 5 or 5.30am, six days a week. I finished at 12.30 and went back in the afternoon to work overtime, which was compulsory in those days, or back in the evening likewise. Things have changed these days as Hitchin is no longer the Head Office taking in Stevenage, Letchworth, Baldock etc. There was always plenty of overtime in those days as much as twenty or thirty hours a week and we were glad to do it as basic wages were very low. In 1946 when I started it was £3 12s 6d; in 1973, when I retired, it was £23 16s Od. Even today they are well below wages in industry. It is only in these times of high unemployment that the Post Office can recruit adequate staff.

Social life was almost non-existent as late nights and early mornings do not go together. I've known the time when I had not seen my children for five days as I had been at work when they got up for school and they were in bed, hopefully asleep, by the time I returned home in the evening. My dear wife did most of the bringing up of the children.

During my time with the PO I made quite a lot of friends, especially around the Stotfold, Holwell and Ickleford areas. The Sutton family at Old Ramerick Farm and Mr Hunter of New Ramerick, the Lawtons, the Lumsdens of the New Inn [*now closed down - SLW*] just to name a few. I am still recognised by most of them and pass the time of day when we meet. Alas as the years roll on they get fewer and fewer.

I finished work with the Post Office in 1973 when great changes were coming in; the modernisation of Post Offices, the advent of automation and the post codes. I have not seen any improvement so far but maybe I am biased.

My next employment was as a security officer with International Computers - but that's another story!

A Relic of the Bancroft House School, Hitchin

P A Clark

The boy this book belonged to was Albert Arundel Hoye, and at the date of the book (1878), he was fourteen years old. He was the younger of the two sons of Arthur Searle Hoye, who was brewer and landlord of the Bedford Arms, Hitchin, and his wife Esther. Arthur Searle Hoye (born 1817), and his wife Esther (nee Hoye, born 1825), were cousins, the children of Thomas Hoye, Merchant, and James Hoye, Gentleman, respectively. As can be seen they are rather old to have a boy of only fourteen, the mother being 53 in 1878, and in fact she died that year.

Right: Albert Hoye's book referred to in this article. (P A Clark)

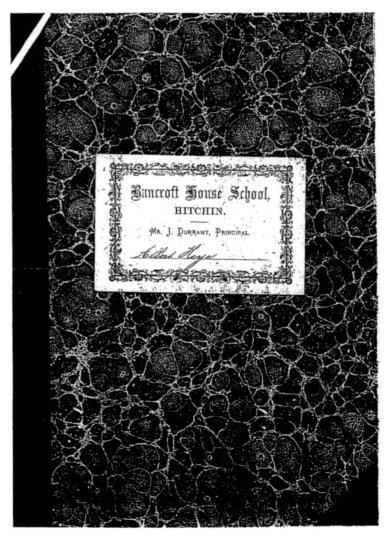

I think that by the year 1880 Arthur must have known, or suspected that he was dying, for he made a will couched in no uncertainty, naming his nephew, Lewis Jarman Hoye, his executor and "Guardian of his infant son". He died on 20 December 1881, almost exactly a year later.

Albert Arundel came under the guardianship of his cousin, at the age of 17, and in the "Inland Revenue - Succession Duty on Real Property" is already called "a brewer". His brother aged nineteen is listed as "a Chemist of Reading, Berks".

Lewis Jarman Hoye appears to have acted as Brewer & Landlord of the Bedford Arms during Albert Arundel's minority, as in the release to his guardianship in 1885 he is listed as publican. Albert Arundel is still listed as brewer, but his brother is now listed as violinist, still of Reading.

Left: the Bedford Arms before its closure. The Hoye family ran this pub from1867-1898, with a brief interlude between 1894-1895 when it was under the management of Joseph Allison. It closed in 2014, and was converted into flats. The pub sign was a black eagle with a castle superimposed on it. (Alan Fleck)

Upon this release, Albert Arundel appears to have taken up the brewing and landlord's roles of his father, and so continued until 1898 when the pub was sold to J W Green Ltd of Luton. Albert was married in 1887 to Elizabeth Atkin, also of Hitchin.

He appears to have retired on leaving the pub at only thirty-four! He died in 1910 aged forty-six. He had six children:

> Albert Percy 1888 - killed 1917
> Arthur Bernard 1889 - died 1890 (tragic accident)
> Violet Amy Helen 1891 - died 1973 (my mother)
> Mabel Constance 1892 - died 1922
> Amelia Dorothea Rose 1896 - died 1984 (?)
> Robert Cecil 1897 - died 1957 (war disabled)

This just about concludes this cameo, but perhaps a word about Elizabeth Atkin (1866 - 1917). She was related through marriage to the Ansell's (butchers) in Moss' Corner. Also it is worth dwelling on the fact that her father was christened "Tom" Atkin.

Bancroft House School

Simon Walker

From the archives of North Hertfordshire Museum Service we have more information about Bancroft House School. The School rules make interesting reading:

R U L E S
of
Bancroft House School, Hitchin.

^^

" It is good for a man to bear the yoke in his youth."

^^

THE PUPILS OF THIS SCHOOL ARE REQUIRED—

1   Not to disturb the work of the school by entering late.
2   Not to be disorderly in the house, school, or bed-rooms.
3   Not to go into the bed-rooms at unusual hours without leave.
4   Not to injure or deface the school premises.
5   Not to leave books or clothes about.
6   Not to wear hats or caps in school.
7   Not to be untidy in personal appearance.
8   Not to throw stones—a most dangerous practice.
9   Not to quarrel with or annoy other boys.
10 Not to play in a violent or dangerous manner.
11 Not to go off the premises without leave.
12 Not to use low words or phrases.
13 Not to tell tales or speak wrongfully of another.
14 Not to use a book or anything belonging to another.
15 Not to meddle with the gas or fire.
16 Not to misbehave themselves at meals.
17 Not to behave ungentlemanly to anyone.
18 Not to scatter waste paper, orange peel, or other litter, about the premises.
19 Not to retire to rest at night. nor to leave the bed-rooms in the morning, without first saying their prayers
20 Not to forget that they are the sons of Christian parents, and, consequently, are bound to obey all Christian precepts; to cherish kind dispositions, and to maintain at all times a most gentlemanly demeanour.

J. DURRANT, Principal.

Above: a Bancroft House School photograph. Unfortunately the year is not recorded. (North Hertfordshire Museum Service).

Part of the School prospectus ran as follows:

J. DURRANT, PRINCIPAL.
(Late Principal of the Hyde Road Schools, Manchester, and formerly Head Master of the Grammar School, Botesdale.)

SYSTEM, DISCIPLINE, AND COURSE OF STUDY.
Mr. DURRANT, from his varied experience in the important work of Education, and from the numerous successes of his Pupils in passing Competitive and other Examinations, can guarantee that the Course of Instruction pursued at BANCROFT HOUSE, will efficiently prepare the Pupils for the active duties of Professional, Agricultural, or Commercial Life, in accordance with the most approved systems of the day. A chief feature in the plan adopted here, is to make the Pupils feel the importance of their Education, and take an interest in their work. Each Pupil receives marks for Conduct and Studies, and takes a position each week according to merit. A spirit of cheerful emulation is thus excited throughout the School, which stimulates to greater exertion, producing industry and self-dependence, and at the same time preventing the necessity of severe discipline.

The General Course of Instruction Comprises the following Subjects :-

1. Scripture History.
2. Reading, Spelling, Dictation.
3. Grammar, Literature, Composition.
4. Arithmetic, Mental Arithmetic, Rapid Calculations.
5. Book-keeping, Invoices, Mercantile Correspondence.
6. Euclid,[1] Algebra, Mensuration.[2]
7. Plain and Ornamental Penmanship.
8. Geography, Mapping, the use of the Globes.
9. Ancient and Modern History.
10. The Natural Sciences, and Elementary Drawing.

The following Subjects are optional according to the wishes of Parents, and the capabilities and requirements of the Pupils:—Practical Land Surveying, Latin, French, Advanced Drawing, Vocal and Instrumental Music, and Dancing.

Vol 10 no 3, October 1995

Past into Present: Hitchin's New Town Hall

David Howlett

The New Town Hall has recently been the subject of public interest again, almost a century after it was first opened. The deliberations of North Hertfordshire District Council have revealed that, because inadequate money has been spent in routine maintenance over the past fifteen or twenty years, important repairs are now needed for which there are insufficient funds. The question has even been raised as to whether we need to retain the New Town Hall at all.

The building is no stranger to controversy. In 1897 Frederic Seebohm and William and Alfred Ransom offered to donate land opposite the Old Town Hall in Brand Street for the erection of Assembly Rooms or Hall for the town. The recently formed Urban District Council decided to build not just the Hall but also a range of offices for its own officials. This was to cost about £4,500.

Some ratepayers were far from happy. During the town council election campaign of 29th March 1899 Francis Newton asked electors "Why have a Town Hall thrust on us when a majority of the Council and Ratepayers do not even like the plan? In spending the public money let us have what we would like, not give way to NON-RATEPAYERS to put up anything to please their fancy!"

---

[1] Geometry.

[2] A branch of mathematics that deals with measurement of various parameters of geometric figures.

Those of Mr Newton's opinion were, however, overruled and the New Town Hall was built at a cost of £7,300. It was opened in March 1901 by Mrs Hudson, wife of Hitchin's MP. The Chairman of the HUDC explained how "... it behove the Council to have regard for the future generations and any slight extra burden should be borne cheerfully and he felt sure that future generations would be grateful for the effort made...." Frederic Seebohm also argued strongly in favour of "a good town hall".

Above: Architect's drawing of the new Town Hall, one of several designs considered. (North Hertfordshire Museum Service)

As we ponder the future of the building perhaps we should think carefully about what Mr Hill and Mr Seebohm said in 1901. Civic pride induced Frederic Seebohm and the Ransom's to give the land; W O Times also presented the plaster work for the Council Chamber (now the Lucas Room) and a memorial tablet was placed near the stage door in honour of Hitchin's medical benefactor Dr Oswald Foster. In 1901, therefore, the Town Hall represented a living portion of the town's identity. It is a great shame that, as "future generations", we have allowed a building which included substantial gifts to the town, to decay to the extent that its future is being seriously questioned.

Vol 10 no 3, October 1995

Hitchin's Lost Landmarks:
Bowman's Mill in Walsworth Road
Sue Fitzpatrick

When Bowman's Mill was built close to Hitchin Station to utilise the railway for its deliveries, it was called Station Mill. (At one time the Bowman family owned at least four mills).

It was pulled down in the 1980s which made many of its previous employees very sad. Olive Watts, now 82, made the tea for the staff for over twenty-five years between 1955 and 1980 when she retired. She began there packing the flour but after three months her husband wanted her to leave lest she should get "flour on your chest".

Olive didn't leave though, and soon she transferred to the canteen. As she says: "They were good days, they really were. It had to be for me to stay there all that time".

As well as Olive's home-made bread pudding sold at 2d a piece, there were other treats, not least her mince pies at Christmas made with Bowman's flour.

Right: Bowman's Mill during its demolition in 1983. It was replaced by a B & Q DIY store; that in turn has given way to B & M Stores. (Terry Wilson)

At one time the mill supplied McVities, Bowman's having discovered an enzyme which softened biscuit flour; more humbly, they also supplied the Victoria pub in Hitchin.

Working with the Bowman family seems to have inspired loyalty and affection. Outings were not uncommon and the staff could buy bags of flour for two shillings (10p in decimal currency) a time.

Olive remembers Rory Bowman, the Managing Director's son, working at the mill during his university vacation and having to clock on and off like everyone else and even arriving on a bicycle. The men started around 7am.

Olive's canteen was housed in an old pub building[1] on the site and she recalls the wonderful views of Hitchin from the uppermost storey of the mill where the flour was sieved through silk. She said "It was an old building but everything was spotless".

To fill her rolls and sandwiches Olive went daily to Day's in Walsworth Road buying fresh cheese and ham. Looking back she says:

"I enjoyed it and I had a wage packet; that was lovely. I used to feel like the Queen of England".

When she left one member of staff was moved to write: "The tea won't taste the same without you".

The mill was built in 1900 and with its outbuildings and yard took up the whole site of what is at the time of writing a B & M store.

Vol 10 no 4, February 1996

Remembering 1945
Extracts from the Autumn Term 1945 Hitchin Grammar
School Chronicle
Blue-Pencilling the Association News, 1939 - 1945

The approach of the first peaceful Christmas for six years and the conclusion of another issue of news of Old Boys provides an appropriate moment for reflection. For this issue is unique in one respect and for a reason which perhaps few of our readers may suspect.

In December 1939, we submitted a typewritten draft of Old Boys' news to the Ministry of Information. The reasons were two-fold: it was important that information of naval and military movements should not reach the enemy, and we at the editorial end had to safeguard ourselves. The script was returned with several deletions, a word blue-pencilled here and there. So through the dark hours of 1940, the better days of 1941 and 1942, the thrilling events of 1942, and so on, until the recent Japanese surrender, two printed copies of

---

[1] The Railway Junction Inn. It had closed in 1962.

the galley-proofs have gone to the Press Censor for the action of his staff. One copy was retained in London and the other censored and always returned promptly within forty-eight hours. Sometimes the excisions seemed fantastic, but experience soon showed us what was required.

The flying bombs of 1944 provided us with a few thorny moments. We soon learnt that, in spite of visual evidence to the contrary, the doodles only came over singly; they never landed in a London suburb, but always in Southern England.   Why should they not, indeed? Such a wide area ought to satisfy everyone in war-time whether it meant Pirton or Peckham.

The submission of news was voluntary, made in a spirit of co-operation to prevent any breach of Security. The Censor asked, however, that no indication of censorship should be given in our columns, a request that tied our hands to some extent.

"Items about Servicemen seem nebulous in character or hazy in statement, but members will understand we have no desire to spend Christmas in the Tower for committing breaches of recent legislation".

So we wrote in 1939. Thanks to the courtesy of the Press Censor, we did not go to the Tower, and we avoided the hang-man's ropes; and, as the other Editor remarks, no noose is good news.

* * * * * *

P A Tomey… writes an interesting account of his movements since last April, when his R A F unit left Holland:-

"We had spent a very enjoyable winter, and it was with great regret we left the country. We crossed the German frontier near Gennep, and reached our site between Sonsbeck and Xanten, places which had received severe batterings from our artillery and aircraft. The latter place was hardly more than heaps of rubble. The few civilians about were wandering aimlessly carrying the few possessions they managed to salvage from the ruins of their homes. Others seemed only interested in looting. After a week there we moved to Osnabruck. From this site we moved to a village on the edge of Luneburg Heath, where the only trees were conifers and heather displaced grass. Although we lived in tents, we did not sleep on the ground, for every one of us had acquired a German service bed. Our football team was still active, and for our away matches we travelled, not in the back of a lorry, but in comfort in a German 'bus, also "found". The departing army unit handed over the keys of the local cinema, and after a few fascinating hours in the projection box we were able to put on regular shows, with a change of film every second day. Eventually we traced the local operator, and he ran the shows for us, for while we were here the surrender took place. We had two celebration parties, one premature (by far the better) and the other official."

"After V E Day we spent most of our spare time watching columns of the Wehrmacht and Luftwaffe travelling along the roads to the concentration areas. We saw convoys of German waggons complete with motor cycle dispatch riders and officers, parked along the roadside, many of these convoys being several miles in length. A few days later we travelled up to Schleswig, crossing the Kiel Canal and passing through Hamburg en route. The bomb damage was the worst we had seen, and the dock area of the city was just a mass of twisted steel and rubble. The first few weeks at Schleswig provided a holiday for us. Our site was beside a lake. We managed to obtain several (German) rubber dinghies and a motor boat. The weather was extremely good, and we spent most of our time boating and bathing. Some of us were lucky enough to go for a trip along the River Schlei on a Luftwaffe air-sea rescue launch manned by the Luftwaffe crew. When the weather changed we moved into billets in Schleswig, a small Luftwaffe camp, the most comfortable place since we had left England. Here entertainment is well organised, with two cinemas and a theatre."

* * * * * *

The First Peace Time Christmas

Father Christmas sat in an icy attic on an upturned orange-box. He sat in an icy attic because he had been unable to find other lodgings his own palace having been blitzed in 1940, and totally wrecked by a succession of flying bombs, V2's and well-meaning but unskilled repair workers. The orange-box he had purchased as a genuine piece of Chippendale Utility furniture, and it had cost him two pounds ten, apart from the three priority dockets, which in their turn had demanded the filling up of numerous forms. Although it was freezing cold, he mopped his brow, for Father Christmas was worried: he sighed profoundly. "So this", he said, "is the first peace-time Christmas for six years", and this was followed by an even deeper sigh. For the word Peace brought back many happy memories to him.

He remembered those old time Christmases, when he was helped by nice, pleasant jocular fathers, who, in hired cloaks and borrowed beards, tried to convince their incredulous offspring that they really had come down the chimney (as if their ample corporations would permit that). Now, alas! although their corporations, no longer ample, but reduced by war-time diet, did permit it, there were no red cloaks or white beards to hire for the love of money. It was all very disappointing, very troublesome. Then Father Christmas remembered those gorgeous, furry, well-built toys, and those amply filled stockings. The thought brought tears to his old rheumatic eyes. He had already expended his meagre funds (income tax, savings weeks and squander bugs had all been busy); he had bought a few pieces of wood, some of them wobbly, others with finnicky funnels, which were supposed to represent tanks, cars, ships and even Meteor jet-planes. The salesman had assured him that this was all that the black market had been able to put up that year, most of the wood being used to make pure Scotch. "Anyway", he had confided, "if you don't have it, the other fools will, and you'll have nothing at all". Tears rolled down Father Christmas's cheek (for he was a dear old gentleman, genuinely fond of kiddies). Apart from that he had managed to buy some

Christmas stockings, crammed with tinfoil, corks and witty mottos; but that was all. And there he sighed once again, still more deeply, for he remembered that his goats (reindeers were unobtainable; the Russians had refused to release any from Finland) had succumbed to temptation, had eaten all the tinfoil, and were now gloriously sick. Apart from that, he had just received a circular from the Father Christmases Union calling for a strike. He did not want to disappoint the kiddies, but he also did not want to let down his fellow Father Christmases. He put his head in his hands, a picture of gloom and misery. Then suddenly, his face brightened; there was, after all, an extra four ounces of sweets and two penn'orth of corned beef!

* * * * * *

The Prisoners of War Return from the Far East

During September and October cables arrived for the relatives of the men who had been in the prisoner-of-war camps of the Japs. Most of these men had been captured at Singapore, and one or two in Malaya, and, though occasionally cards had arrived, all very much out-of-date, official announcements had given people at home some qualms as to the actual position, indeed as to the actual safety of these prisoners. The arrival of the good news, and, better still, the home-coming of the returned men one by one during October and early November, brought all the more joy to those who had waited so long for them.

The list of the returned Old Boys includes:- E R Bowskill, D Chandler, R R Childs, G A Hancock, J H Martin, G W Mott, H Muncey, F Pearmain, G L Thomas, J M Thomson.

We have read somewhere that the construction of the Thailand railway cost one man per sleeper. Some of the above men had been working for years on the railway, saving enough from their meagre pittance to purchase essentials. All told of the inhumanity of the "Nips", of cruelty and starvation.

Frank Pearmain came along to the Old Boys' Day looking as if he had made a quick recovery after his experiences on the railway. He confessed to being an expert at skinning and frying lizards and snakes.

We saw Reginald Childs for a brief moment. He looked fairly well and made the comment that the stories about the Japs were only too true.

Graham Thomas has been suffering from pneumonia and pleurisy, but we understand he has turned the corner. We wish him a speedy recovery.

John H Martin's return was especially welcome, and he has made good progress since his release.

Herbert Muncey, like Frank Pearmain, worked on the railway and spoke of a seven-day week, and a very long day at that, with a meagre diet of rice.

John McP Thomson travelled more widely than the others. He saw service in Palestine and in Malaya, where he was captured. He finished up in a Korean camp and was ultimately released by the Russians and given a welcome that included food and vodka. He writes that he is in excellent health.

Vol 11 no 4, March 1999

Transport in Hitchin in the 1940s - 50s

Birch Brothers operated a very popular coach service from Rushden, Northants to London, Kings Cross and return every hour seven days a week. Thousands of personnel were transported from local RAF stations into Hitchin and Kings Cross. Huge six wheeled and heavy double deck coaches always travelled spot on time. These coaches came into Hitchin via Blake's Corner opposite Bancroft recreation ground, Bancroft and out via Sun Street.

The latest coaches were built for the Festival of Britain in 1951 and were called the "Marlborough". Each coach was called after members of the House of Marlborough; for instance "Winston Churchill" etc. The coaches were massive, over fifteen feet high and more than eight feet wide, very safe to drive and comfortable for the passengers.

After leaving the stop opposite Woolworth's for London, drivers had not only to negotiate the old market square but line their coaches up to pass in between Curry's and The Angel Public House.

Above: The Angel Vaults *in Sun Street, formerly* The Angel. *(Hitchin Historical Society)*

They had to be careful to miss the overhanging shop and pub signs (inches were very important) then down into Sun Street where it was more than possible they would meet other Birch Bros. coaches coming into Hitchin from London. Passengers could look down from the top deck into the bedroom windows. I was on my way to work one morning and talking to the milkman when, all of a sudden, just behind us the old Angel pub fell down; we were lucky not to be under it.

If the service coach started to fill up the conductor or an inspector would telephone control and immediately the manager, Mr (Paddy) Walsh, would send out stand by crews with a spare coach.

Following driving for Birch Brothers I started working for London Transport. Opposite Massey's timber yard in Stevenage Road was a small shop where I used to buy drinks and eats. It is now 161 Stevenage Road.

D T Larkins

[Woolworth's was in the High Street, in the building now occupied by Boots Chemist. The Angel didn't just "fall down"; it was sadly demolished in 1956. It was a McMullens pub; I've often wondered why they were permitted to destroy such and ancient building – it was mid-15th century. SLW]

Vol 11 no 4, March 1999

Hitchin: Childhood Memories of the 1920s and 30s
Marshall F Dellar

No television! A radio if you were lucky, though they were not very good in those days. An occasional trip to the cinema to watch silent films with a pianist playing the accompaniment loud or soft according to how exciting the action was. One of the films we watched was called "Rin Tin Tin", the name of the star, which was a German shepherd dog. These films were the forerunner of todays' "soaps" and left us each week with a cliff-hanger making sure we would attend the following week to see if he had escaped his predicament. Photography was black and white in those days; colour would come many years later although when one looks at some of the old photographs they were excellently done.

Depending on the time of year we would decide what we would do. For instance in the spring and summer we would go for long walks in the countryside and pick large bunches of cowslips and primroses and later armfuls of bluebells. Nowadays it is against the law to pick wild flowers but no pesticides or other chemicals were used to enhance the growing of crops. Remember the kind of grass we used to collect called "Quaking" grass? It was said that if you could hold the grass still it would turn to gold. One of the very few places where one could find it growing was in a hollow in Priory Park and also at the top of Tatmore Hill.

At a place called Target we used to gather wild strawberries in abundance, the taste and flavour of which was absolutely delicious. In the autumn we picked bags of blackberries or crab apples for mother to make jams and jellies. Sloes for making sloe gin was another favourite as were hazelnuts and filberts.

In the evenings we would sit indoors and play games such as snakes and ladders, draughts and Ludo, not forgetting playing cards and dominoes. The latter was played in most public houses in those days though no money was allowed as any sort of gambling was very much forbidden. If you lost a game you could buy the victor a half or a pint of beer or such like.

We didn't have many toys. The girls would have dolls for which they made clothes from odd scraps of materials and pieces of lace. For the boys it was tops and hoops. The best hoop was made of steel and had a metal hook to drive it along. Running about with it gave us plenty of exercise.

During school days we were taught the three R's. The boys were also given lessons in gardening, a much loved task and of continuing use to this day. Woodwork and metalwork were also taught using basic tools and equipment. The girls were taught needlework, embroidery and cooking skills. School on the whole was quite enjoyable although very strict. This was good when you compare things as they are today. The crime rate was low and the ordinary person had respect for other people's property. Not that we were angels but you could walk about day or night without fear of being molested. Houses were seldom, if ever, locked up.

I remember when St Mary's Square was just heaps of rubble and the river was a muddy old stream running through. It was soon to be transformed into the delightful square we have today, a great asset to the beauty of the town.

There was also Mr Brownlow the butcher who had a slaughter house at the top of Biggin Lane. We used to stand and watch him put the finishing touches to the poor animals, some of whom were on their last legs, but it provided cheap meat to the poorer people of the neighbourhood.

Going back to the development of the square and the river; fed by chalk springs at Well Head in Charlton, the water used to bubble out of the bottom of a lovely crystal clear pool and flow towards Hitchin. It was joined en route by other springs at the bottom end of Priory Park near The Windmill public house. A working water wheel was in situ at Grey's farm in the village and the remains of the wheel can still be seen through the fence.

Returning to the pool where the springs were, I remember the lovely fish which swam there. These have long perished since the pumping station started at Well Head. The river used to run towards Charlton through the meadows where it divided in two, creating an island with the water backing up to the water mill.

It is not commonly known that the springs were some distance from the road along a farm track and just a couple of hundred yards beyond the ford at Ingrey's farm, hidden by trees from the track. Going further along the road to the next turning on the left brings you to the bottom of the hill we used to call the Pinnacle. It was steep hill where cowslips, primroses and violets grew in abundance.

Another of my childhood memories of Purwell, where I live now, is of the meadows with the small river running through. Let's start where the river really begins in the woods at the Stevenage Road side of St Ippollits.[1] The springs bubble out of the ground there and make their way to the bottom of Whitehill where it passes under Stevenage Road. The river at this point is called The Riddy. It continues along the bottom of the Oakfield Estate to the railway embankment. Just before it goes under the railway it is joined by another stream called Ashbrook. When it comes out the other side of the railway the brook passes under Wymondley Road and continues along the edge of St Michael's estate. Today a nice tarmac path runs alongside the river. The real Ninesprings rise in a fishing lake known as Coots' Corner and the water is discharged through two large outlet pipes into the brook about five hundred yards from the Wymondley Road. Over the years the flow from the lake has never stopped, not even during the last severe drought.

At this point the river is called the Purwell. A further two hundred yards on it is joined by another spring bubbling up in the Purwell woods and continues on its way until it reaches the Purwell mill. Here at one time the water was controlled by gates or dams to allow the mill to work which I believe it did until the 1920's. The river continues across the meadows to Cambridge Road bridge adjacent to the Millstream public house, formerly called The Ship Inn. Just before it arrives at this point more springs join the river in what used to be the watercress beds. The beds were once farmed by the Sansom family of Whitwell who still grow watercress today. The river now passes under the road and continues across Walsworth Common, under the railway and out into Grove Road where it meets the River Hiz. It provides a very pleasant walk in the summer and quite a few birds can be seen including the occasional kingfisher, woodpecker and many other species: even herons are sometimes to be seen.

I remember the Boys' Club in the old tithe barn in Tilehouse Street at the rear of Shadbolt's shop. Many happy hours were spent there in my early teens but time was passing rapidly by and World War Two was upon us. The only way we could keep the club going was to open the doors to the troops stationed in the town. It provided somewhere they could pop in and have a cup of tea. Later the club was closed and we would meet in the stables at Lewisford House in Upper Tilehouse Street. This did not last long either and the club was again re-located to Walsworth Road. This was also used by the military as a troops' canteen and

---

[1] The 1881 Census records no less than 28 different spellings of St Ippolyts!

shared by the Boys' Club. Run by Mr Tom Baldry, who used to help at Tilehouse Street, it continued for many years. It was about this time I volunteered for the Royal Navy and didn't see the Youth or Boys' Club for several years.

One further memory is of the airship R101 on its fateful last journey as it passed over the cemetery in St John's Road. It was not very high and I had a very good view. I was later to learn that it had crashed in France with catastrophic loss of life. That was the end of the airship as a long distance mode of travel.

Above: the R101 at its mooring mast at Cardington. It's hard to get an idea of just how big she was, at 223 metres (731ft) in length. The two airship sheds remain at Cardington, and to go inside them is a true experience. (Image: public domain)

Christmas always brings fond memories of the ham on the boil in the copper; what a lovely smell! We were not very well off but somehow we always lived well at this time of the year and also at Easter. There would be a large jar of ginger in syrup and dates, figs and nuts which was quite a treat. Dinner on Christmas Day was usually a large farmyard hen with all the trimmings. This was followed by Christmas pudding with silver threepenny pieces in it for the children to find. No doubt these were a bribe to make us eat some. Later in the afternoon it was Christmas tea with all the family attending. Boiled ham with pickles, Christmas cake which dad always iced, followed by fruit trifle and cream. After tea we played the usual party games with forfeits to pay until it was time for bed. All the pickles, trifles etc. were home-made. The whole ham and ginger came from Halsey's in Churchyard where mother used to buy her groceries. She used to pay sixpence a week into a club which was enough at Christmas and Easter to pay for the ham and a few other goodies.

Alas my wrist tires but I hope this narrative shows a little of life in Hitchin and kindles fond memories of the twenties and thirties.

Vol 11 no 4, March 1999

Memories of Tilehouse Street

Ken Boxall

I was born on the 9th September 1918 at number 21 Bucklersbury, Hitchin. My father, Henry William, known to friends and family as Bill, was still serving in the Royal Naval Air Force[1] soon to become the Royal Air Force. He remained in the service until 1920 on the advice of his family because there was very little work available. On returning to civvy street we moved to number 83 Tilehouse Street which is situated between the Coopers Arms public house and the big house of number 84 then occupied by the Wright family and the landlord of number 83. Next door to and adjoining the pub were two small houses which were tenanted by the Spencers and Haggars. One neighbour was in the habit of using impolite language and I, being only two years of age, was heard to repeat phrases like "you old bubber" which my mother did not find amusing. The house had a cobbled back yard with an out-building which housed coal etc., and in which my mother did the washing. In the centre of the right hand side was a well, unused and blanked off, from which would emerge the occasional frog which were not a nuisance unless they hopped through the back door. An occasional rat had been seen in this yard and my father brought home a powerful airgun to deal with it.

It happened one day that staying with us was a friend of my mother's with her small son. She was a wonderful pianist and used to enthral our family playing our piano which my mother played because she was a natural untrained pianist who would listen to a tune played on the radio and play it immediately on the piano. I digress! It was while this friend

---

[1] The Royal Naval Air Service was the aeronautical wing of the Royal Navy. It was merged with the Royal Flying Corps (the army equivalent) on1 April 1918 as the Royal Air Force. In 1924 the Fleet Air Arm (still part of the RAF) was formed; and on 24 May 1939 the Fleet Air Arm was returned to Admiralty control. (SLW)

was staying with us that this rat appeared. My mother's friend picked up the rifle and with a single shot killed it. What a woman!

At that time Tilehouse Street, although always a busy street for traffic, was a family street with a family occupying each house including the "Tile House". This was occupied by the Nicholls who owned the jam factory which stood on the site of the Midland Bank building prior to it being occupied by the Fosters, the local builders, as a yard for storing materials. Up the street from us was Cooper's, the butchers, who kept animals for slaughter in the meadow now the site of Minsden. It was quite a common sight to see animals being driven down Wratten Road and up Tilehouse Street to Cooper's where they would be slaughtered.

In 1930 my father felt the need for a larger house and we moved down the road to number 18 which was situated on the corner of Wratten Road. This was a large three storey house with four bedrooms, a boxroom and a cellar which had racks for wine storage. Most of the houses in Tilehouse Street had cellars. Through one of the bedrooms ran a steel bar to stop the walls from bulging. I thought it was there for me to swing on like a trapeze, let go and land on the bed, but woe betide me if dad caught me at it. Being a corner house it had a gas lamp attached which had to be lit by a man from the gas company each night. The putting out of this light would frequently wake me but I soon went back to sleep again. You did in those days, for as I remarked earlier the traffic from heavy lorries rumbling their way from the growing fields of the fens to Covent Garden through the night was something you got used to.

On the opposite side of the street was a second-hand furniture shop owned by the Furr family. Old Mr Furr, a lovely old man, father of the generation of Furrs still living locally, loved the children who lived in the street and had a favourite expression. He would say to me, "Hello Will, had your whittles?"[1] an old fashioned phrase heard no more. Next door to Furr's was the sweet shop owned by the Lamb family and thereby hang grim memories for under the shop was a cellar with gratings in the street. There were a lot of horses working in those days and it happened one day that a horse drawing a cart bolted from fright and as it came down Wratten Road tried to turn down Tilehouse Street towards Bucklersbury. The poor creature failed, slipped down the road and fell with its front legs down the gratings of the sweet shop. The owner of the horse arrived and a vet was sent for. There was no way the horse could be got out and so the slaughterman from Cooper's the butchers was sent for, a Mr Knight. At that time there were no humane killers and Mr Knight killed the horse with a slaughterman's pick-axe. Another horse drawn vehicle from Ickleford arrived with a low loader cart and a winch to haul the body away.

Behind our house in Wratten Road was a very high wall enclosing the kitchen garden of Doctor Foster who lived at number 13. We played all sorts of ball games against this wall and

---

[1] I can only assume this to be a dialect version of "victuals", pronounced "vittles". [SLW]

needless to say they frequently went over. There were arguments as to who should knock on Doctor Foster's door to ask if we could get them back. As often as not the door was opened by Mrs Foster, a gracious lady if ever there was one, tall, beautifully spoken and everlastingly tolerant to our requests. She and her husband graced our street, a wonderful couple. In the days before the National Health Service no cut was too small for him to look at. I recall being bitten by one of the dogs which used to run around, he took me into his surgery, lit a match to cauterise the bite and treated me with the utmost gentleness not usually given to small boys.

Down the street at number 11 lived the Hardings who sold newspapers, magazines and comics. If I had been good, dad would give me tuppence and I would run down to Harding's shop and spend it on *The Rover* or *Adventure*. George Day lived next door at number 12. The Days were another family who made their living in the street. George Day was the last real basket maker for miles around and his son, also called George, was one of the boys in the street. He was killed early in the Second World War.

Right: Harding's Newsagents in the 1930s. It remained a newsagents at least until the 1970s. The building had previously been the Three Tuns public house; it is now a private one! (Simon Walker)

Above: the Three Tuns when it was still a pub, selling the ales of J W Green Ltd Luton (SLW)

85

Opposite the Days dwelt Mrs Taylor the bakers, later to become Bliss Bros Bakers. Mrs Taylor's penny ice buns were scrumptious. Further down the road, on the corner of Bucklersbury and Tilehouse Street, there was a grocers and wine shop called Barnabas Russell. Almost daily it seemed I was sent running for a pound of sugar or a packet of biscuits which you could often buy loose and cheaply if they were broken. When I accompanied my mother to shop, primarily to carry her basket home, I would be fascinated when the man behind the counter carved a piece of butter from a large lump and patted it about with two wooden "patters" which he dipped in water to stop them sticking, eventually to end up with a nice shaped portion which usually weighed what my mother had asked for. Similarly the cheese was cut with a wire with a toggle on the end, a system which still prevails behind the scenes in supermarkets today.

Opposite the grocers and up the yard was the old tithe barn which housed the boys' club. No sex liberation in those days, the girls had to have their own club but I can't remember where it was if there was one. From this base we occupied ourselves in the winter evenings occasionally having a paper chase round the town or a cross country run, usually round the back of Charlton village and Gosmore, about three to four miles. Boxing gloves were available and this was the place to have a go at anyone whom you had a grudge against and under proper supervision you got it out of your system with the two contestants normally finishing up good pals. My only grudge match was against a lad who was in the same office where I had just started work at the age of fourteen and a half. He resented the attention I was receiving from a young lady in the office. The fight was going against me and was stopped but I had the satisfaction of being unmarked whereas he had a very red nose to show.

The years were passing. My mother had a new kitchen built with a gas cooker fitted and so did not have to light a fire in the grate in the mornings in order to cook the breakfast. About this time a wonderful thing happened. One evening my father came in and called me downstairs from my bed. On the table he had a shoe box in which rested a Bakelite sheet about eighteen inches square. On it was mounted various electrical coils and three glass bulbs which he called valves. He connected this base to a big dry battery, a small dry battery and a sort of glass box he called an accumulator. After screwing in various switches music came out of a large brass trumpet mounted vertically. It had been made by an acquaintance of my father's, Mr Dellar and father of Mr Dellar still living in the town. This was our first radio though we called it a wireless set!

In the mid-thirties I was old enough to ride a motor bike. Two of the boys in the street already had one but they were two years older than I. When I saw a James two-stroke motor cycle for sale at Morgans in Sun Street I had to have it. At fourteen pounds a real bargain!

By now the ravages of time were telling on our house and my father decided to buy one instead of renting as previously. He would have liked a house in Offley Road but it was £750 and more than he could afford in weekly payments. He did find a nice family house in Trevor Road which was only £650 so we moved and our connections with a lovely old street where so many happy years had been spent was severed.

Vol 12 no 1, October 1999

Malting And Brewing In Hitchin

Allan Whitaker

Hitchin is an old market town which was also on a number of important horse and coach routes during the eighteenth and nineteenth centuries which led to the establishment of approximately one hundred inns and beerhouses. A number of breweries were built in the town to deal with the demand for beer. The raw materials for brewing are malt (from barley), hops, a reliable source of water, yeast and possibly other adjuncts. Good malting barley was readily available from local farms in Hertfordshire. In 1742, Samuel Whitbread who was brewing in London rented a malting in Hitchin (site not known) to obtain high quality malt for his brewery.

In the malthouses the barley was steeped (soaked) in water for two to three days. Then it was allowed to germinate on tiled floors under controlled conditions to convert the starch in the grains to the sugars the brewer required. At the correct stage the 'green barley' was placed on a fine wire mesh in a kiln above a furnace in order to dry the grain to prevent any further biochemical changes without destroying enzymes in the grain. The malted barley was then cooled, bagged and stored for future use.

The malthouses in Hitchin were owned by the breweries or independent maltsters. Using Merrett's 1818 map, the tithe map of 1844 and later ordnance survey maps, it has been possible to identify 20 maltings in Hitchin of which only two now remain which are used for other purposes.

Maltings owned by the breweries:-

1. Two malthouses in Bridge St owned by Henry Crabb in 1818, pulled down in 1972 and now occupied by an office block called The Maltings.
2. One malthouse in Tilehouse St (plot 291) in 1844 opposite 25 Tilehouse Street which was owned by Henry Crabb.
3. One malthouse behind 92 Bancroft. In 1818 the owner was Mary Crabb and the tenant was Henry Crabb.
4. Two malthouses in Wratten Rd. In 1818 these were owned by William Lucas. They were eventually pulled down in the 1960s and the site is now occupied by an office block.

5.   One malthouse behind 25 Tilehouse St owned by William Lucas in 1898. This has now been demolished.

6.   One malthouse behind 10 High St (plot 257) originally owned by the Lucas family and in 1818 it was owned by H. J. G. Smith. It was not shown on later maps.

7.   One malthouse at the junction of Walsworth Rd and Nightingale Rd. In 1898 it was owned by William Lucas. In 1901 Bowmans used the site for building a flour mill. Traces of the malthouse tiled floor remained within the mill complex. The site has since been completely redeveloped and it is now owned by B & M as a large retail store.

8.   A possible malthouse on the Lucas brewery site at the corner of Bridge St and Sun St which might have been originally built by the Draper family. Old photographs in Hitchin Museum of the brewery show windows facing Bridge St as being typical of a malting.

9.   One malthouse at the rear of The Sun. This was used by William Hill and shown on the 1844 and 1898 maps.

Maltings owned by independent maltsters:-

10. Two malthouses between the Corn Exchange and The Swan. In 1818 they were owned by Charles Baron and sundry tenants. These were pulled down after 1898.

11. One malthouse behind Bucklersbury on plot 271 in 1818 (now part of Brooker's yard). It was owned and tenanted by Mary Corrie but it is not shown on later maps.

12. One small malthouse behind Churchyard on plot 186 in 1818 (behind Simmons shop). The owner was George Whittingstall and the tenant was Daniel Brown.

13. One malthouse behind Bancroft on plot 190 in 1818. This site is now occupied by Hermitage Road. The owner was William Wilshere and the tenant was Samuel Smith.

14. One malthouse behind Bancroft (Ransoms yard). In 1818 it was owned by Richard Watson and in the 1840's by Susannah Watson. The building is still standing and part of it is used by Ransoms as their boardroom.

15. One malthouse behind 84 and 85 Bancroft, next to the Skynner almshouses. In 1818 it was owned by Thomas Ward and tenanted by Ward and Bailey.

16. Two malthouses on plots 232 and 233 in Bancroft to the south of Regal Chambers and opposite the Skynner almshouses. In 1818 these were owned and tenanted by I. J. Pierson.

17. One malthouse in the yard behind 23 Bancroft (currently The Brickyard bar). John Margetts Pierson was occupying the malthouse in 1794. The malthouse is still standing in a modified form and put to other uses.

18. One malthouse on plot 253 behind Brand St now occupied by the Town Hall. In 1818 it was owned by George Beaver with sundry tenants.

19. One malthouse to the south of The Lord Lister Hotel on plot 352. In 1818 it was owned by James Kidman with sundry tenants.

20. One malthouse in Queen St on the site of the Queen St school. It was used as a malthouse before 1818 when owned by William Wilshere. It was then donated by William Wilshere to be used as a school building for girls and infants. The building which replaced it dates from 1857. Traces of the original brick floor and walls, dating from circa 1700, still remain in the boiler house built in 1837.

Between 1850 and 1900 the majority of these maltings ceased to operate as larger and more economically efficient malthouses were built in Baldock, Bishop's Stortford, Hertford, Sawbridgeworth and Ware. Even the Lucas family who were brewing in Hitchin until 1921 seem to have given up using most of their own malthouses by 1900.

Although brewing probably began in Hitchin in medieval times, the first quoted brewer was Thomas Draper. He was fined in 1602 for operating an unlicensed brewhouse. In 1632 a descendant Benjamin Draper was an active brewer and in 1695 Edward Draper was leasing property and a malting in Sun St, and had leased The Angel and The Chequer. William Conquest began brewing in the market square behind The Red Lion about 1700. He was landlord of The Sun in 1707 (which later had its own brewery) and also owned The Six Bells in Baldock which he sold in 1729. His son John also became a brewer and took over the business.

In 1685, the Lucas family, who were farmers, bankers and maltsters were living in Bancroft with a malting behind the house. By 1709 William Lucas had started brewing at an unknown location and formed a partnership with his brother-in-law Isaac Gray.

In 1734, John Draper, his wife Anne, together with their daughter Elizabeth and son-in-law John Conquest collectively took out a loan for £1,100 from William Lucas. As security they promised the brewery in Sun Street, maltings, barns, outhouses and 48 acres of land in the manor of Hitchin. Unfortunately they were unable to repay the loan and the Lucas family acquired various properties previously owned by the Drapers and Conquests.

By 1748 the Lucas family still had the malthouse, barns and a shop in the High St but also a brewhouse, malthouse and five cottages in Sun St plus freehold, leasehold and copyhold property in Hitchin, St Ippolyts, Datchworth, Offley, Willian, Shefford and Clifton. In 1771 the brewery was rebuilt and at a later stage included buildings for brewing, storage of beer, a cooperage, cask and bottle washing and mineral water production. The five cottages next to the brewery were replaced by a single large house circa 1780. The early tied estate in Hitchin gradually increased and included *The Angel, Bull's Head, Crown, Dial, Half Moon, King's Head, Plough, Red Lion, Ship, Swan with Two Necks, Two Brewers* and *Wheatsheaf*. The brewery operated for another 50 years maintaining a tied estate of approximately 50 tied public houses but never acquired any public houses or beerhouses in Ashwell, Baldock, Royston or Stevenage. Most of the tied estate outside Hitchin was in villages in North Hertfordshire or South Bedfordshire. In 1920 the brewery and associated property were put up for sale. This included *the Adam and Eve, Bricklayers Arms, Crown, Half Moon, Highlander, King's Arms, King's Head, Plough and Dial, Post Boy, Railway Hotel, Railway Junction* and *Rose and Crown* (leasehold) in Hitchin. J. W. Green Ltd. of Luton bought the business in 1921 and closed the brewery in 1923. The brewery buildings were finally demolished in 1963 and replaced by shops and Crown House (now in turn demolished - SLW). All that now remains is the Brewery House in Sun St (now Mevan) and the Tilehouse at 25 Tilehouse St with stones in the archways defining Lucas property boundaries.

John Crabb was brewing at 5 Sun St in a yard behind a Georgian house until he died in 1782. He was followed by his son John Crabb II who died in 1811. His successor, John Crabb III died suddenly aged 25 in 1813 and John II's widow Mary, who also owned a malthouse in Bancroft, remained in charge of the brewery until she died in 1826. In 1823 she had formed a business partnership with John Marshall who was the brewery manager. By this time the Crabb family had built up their tied estate to about 20 public houses which included *the Adam and Eve, Currier's Arms, Highlander, Red Hart* and *Rose and Crown* (leasehold) in Hitchin. In 1832 John Marshall formed a partnership with Joseph Margetts Pierson and soon afterwards he had been replaced by his son John Marshall II. The business prospered and was brewing 5500 barrels annually and had ten rooms, cooler rooms; a cooperage, engine room, vat room, counting house, cask shed, stores and a hop loft plus a commodious family residence with extensive cellarage. The tied estate had increased to at least 46 properties extending over a wide area. In Hitchin they owned *the Adam and Eve, Boot, Cock, Cross Keys, Currier's Arms, Red Cow, Red Hart, Robin Hood, Sailor, Six Bells, Three Horseshoes, Three Tuns, Wellington* and *White Lion.*

Unfortunately Marshall and Pierson joined a speculative alkali works venture in Brussels which failed in 1841 and they were forced to sell the brewery and tied estate. Many of the local brewers bought the inns and beerhouses. Now only the old brewery house (formerly the Hitchin Conservative Association, now the Angel) and a coach house in the yard at the back remain.

One year later in 1842 Joseph Pierson (son of Joseph Margetts Pierson) built the small Bucklersbury brewery on the western corner of Bucklersbury and Tilehouse St. The brewery tap was known as *The Woodman* (20 Bucklersbury) with a 5 quarter brewery at the rear in the yard where he also worked as a coal merchant. He acquired several public houses and beer houses including *The Dog* in Brand St which was pulled down when Sainsbury's shop was built in 1972. He sold the brewery and tied estate when he decided to leave the country in 1852. *The Woodman* building still remains with an altered ground floor that is occupied by shops and offices but there is no trace of the brewery in the yard.

Other small breweries are known to have been in the yard of *The Sun* up to 1902 (now hotel bedrooms), in Portmill Lane in 1836 (now a public car park), in Tilehouse St opposite the Tilehouse in 1860, at *The Peacock* in Queen St from 1850 to 1900 and at *The Bedford Arms* in Bedford Rd from 1866 to 1886.

Note: Plot numbers quoted in the text refer to tithe numbers on the 1818 and 1844 maps.

References

Merrett H. S. (1818). Plan of the town and parish of Hitchin in the county of Hertfordshire, including the hamlets of Walsworth and Preston and Langley. Hitchin Museum.

Hitchin tithe map and award (1814). Diocese of St Albans. County Archives. Hertford Ordnance Survey map of Hitchin (1898)

Poole, H. (1984) *Here for the Beer - A Gazetteer of the Brewers of Hertfordshire*. Watford Museum.

Acknowledgements

Hertfordshire County Archives, Hertford.

Hitchin Museum

Whitbread Archives, London

Ken Page, Brewery Historian

[Allan Whitaker is author of *Brewers in Hertfordshire*, Hertfordshire Publications (2005) ISBN-13: 978-0954218973]

[It is interesting to consider how many pubs referred to in the above article remain open:

PUB NAME	CURRENT STATUS	PUB NAME	CURRENT STATUS
Adam and Eve	closed	Post Boy	closed
Angel	closed	Railway Hotel	closed
Bedford Arms	closed	Railway Junction	closed
Boot	closed	Red Cow	closed
Bricklayers Arms	open	Red Hart	open
Bull's Head	closed	Red Lion	closed
Chequers	closed	Robin Hood	closed
Cock	open	Rose and Crown	open
Cross Keys	closed	Sailor	closed
Crown	closed	Ship (now the Millstream)	open
Currier's Arms	closed	Six Bells, Baldock	closed
Dial	closed	Sun	open
Dog	closed	Swan with Two Necks	closed

Half Moon	open	Three Horseshoes	closed
Highlander	open	Three Tuns	closed
King's Arms	closed	Two Brewers	closed
King's Head	closed	Wellington	closed
Peacock	closed	Wheatsheaf	closed
Plough	closed	White Lion	closed
Plough and Dial	closed	Woodman	closed

Answer: six out of a total of forty. SLW]

Vol 12 no 2, October 2001

A 'Company Servant' on the London and North Eastern Railway in the 1930s

I joined the London and North Eastern Railway in 1936. The Company was very keen on education in those days. Having gained a School Certificate (Exempt London Matric) at Hitchin Boys Grammar School I was graciously excused the railway clerical entry examination.

My first job was at Stevenage station, long since demolished.[1] The booking office entrance was in Julian's Road high above the platforms which were served by an over bridge and two fairly steep flights of stairs.

Curiously enough my longstanding recollection of working there is not the booking office duties but the re-painting of the office (undertaken by painters from the large engineering depot at Hitchin). I watched, fascinated as Mr Bullard, the foreman, transformed our old deal cupboards into beautifully grained wood. Cleaned down, a coat of varnish and, whilst still wet, the careful use of his thumb and a few tools achieved a remarkable result. He was one of the many craftsmen of all trades in the depot at Hitchin electricians, gas fitters, carpenters, painters, blacksmiths etc., responsible for maintenance and repairs at stations and depots over a wide area. Another recollection, again nothing to do with work, is the joy of a senior booking clerk having become a member of Knebworth Golf Club after undergoing a severe scrutiny as to his suitability.

I was, after a short stay, moved to Hatfield Booking Office and then to Hitchin. At Hatfield in that year the Hertfordshire Show was held in the grounds of Hatfield House and I recall seeing Bertram Mills[2] drive his own coach and horses to open the show. As the railway carried much of the goods and show livestock we had free entrance tickets — I spent my

---

[1] Stevenage station was relocated in 1973, better to serve Stevenage New Town.

[2] Bertram Mills was proprietor of Bertram Mills' Circus. Bertram died in 1938, and his sons, Bernard and Cyril took over. The circus continued in operation into the 1960s (with a break during the War years).

lunch hour, economically, lunching on free samples of Horlicks, Ovaltine, various cereals, soft drinks etc... in the afternoon I felt a bit off colour!

Local stations were very busy in those days. Clerks worked a 48 hour week, plus Sunday, undertaking early and late turns of duty (usually one man alone) covering from around 6 a.m. to 11 p.m. Monday to Saturday. All staff were "company servants" and clerks of all grades addressed each other as "Mister." Not "Mr Brown" – just "Mister." Forenames were rarely used unless you had worked with someone for a long time.

Clerical staff were granted two weeks holiday a year which, in the light of general working conditions was good. The bad news was that all leave was allocated by head office for the whole district over the period April to October in rotation. It could be a long time from the first two weeks in April of one year to the last two weeks in October of the next year especially if both were cold and wet. An actual summer holiday was something to look forward to. There was some consolation in working late turns, especially in winter, in that hours of daylight could be enjoyed in the mornings and this could be a reason why so many railwaymen were keen gardeners and allotment holders.

The basic salary scale for clerical staff (class 5) rose in annual increments of 10s to £3 16s 9d per week at age 32. There was little chance of promotion (especially at stations and offices outside London) and many clerks retired at age 60 still on the basic salary. However, it must be said that the railway was a safe and steady job in those pre-war days of depression and, helped by overtime and Sunday duty, prudent staff were even able to save and secure a mortgage. I recall one of my colleagues at Hitchin buying a house on the east side of Cambridge Road price, I think, £650, deposit £90. Larger houses on the other side of the road were priced at £700, deposit £100 which he thought to be beyond his means. Reverting to salaries, I was fortunate in gaining an early promotion to head office and was regarded as a "boy wonder" in gaining a further promotion before I was 32. Alas, I did not continue at that pace although I had many different jobs before reaching British Railway Board Headquarters from whence I retired.

The LNER were very reluctant to pay senior staff at stations to work overtime or Sunday duty. Whilst I was a probationary clerk at Hitchin a letter came from the District Passenger Manager (155 Bishopsgate in the City of London) weekly, enquiring if I was sufficiently trained to take Sunday duty alone. As soon as the Chief Clerk said yes he was instructed to roster me for the next week. (NB. 06:30 — 23:00 hrs, ½ hr for lunch, 16 hours at one shilling and three pence per hour = £1).

The booking and parcels office staff at Hitchin Station in the 1930s were — Chief Clerk (Class 3), 2 senior booking clerks (Class 4) and 3 clerks (Class 5). The three clerks covered in shifts, early turn parcels office, late turn parcels office, middle turn pay bills and also cover during the middle of the day for the senior booking clerks who worked shifts around 05:00 — 13:00 hrs and 16:00 — 24:00 hrs. The pay bills covered booking office staff, goods office staff (in Nightingale Road), station uniformed staff (the Station Master, 3 inspectors, 2 leading porters and other porters, passenger guards and goods guards). Some time sheets, especially for guards were quite involved, with extended hours due to delays or special working and differing rates of pay for ordinary working, overtime, night duty, night duty overtime, Sunday duty and others I can't recall. What I do recall quite clearly is that when the pay bill clerk had finally sorted out all the various spells of duty over a seven day period and reached a grand total of hours and minutes worked, the total minutes never amounted to 7, 22, 37, 52. Why not? Because seven minutes would be dropped, 8 minutes would count as fifteen! What a coincidence — or was it? Arithmetic had been well taught in those days! When I first started, pay bills had to be prepared and forwarded to the Treasurer at Kings Cross for checking. They were returned on Friday with the money to pay out. In later years we were authorised to deal with a local bank — the Chief Clerk took a taxi (almost certainly Boxall) to collect the cash on Friday morning — then a hard stint — all hands engaged to meet a 12 o'clock deadline to pay out — put the money in the envelopes previously prepared with the name and amount — disaster if we didn't balance, cash left over or cash short. All envelopes had to be emptied and cash counted as we paid out (no — the queue was always on time). There were some men who would not accept an unsealed envelope! We were often requested to seal it so that it could be taken home and presented to "the Missus" intact!

My other main job at Hitchin for two weeks out of three was in the parcels office situated behind the new modernised booking office-wide desk (you either stood or perched on a high stool) and in the winter a roaring coal fire (strictly forbidden to fill a scuttle with coal from an engine standing in the platform but the high quality coal was really something to warm you).

Living near the station I go there from time to time to travel and look around. Looking at the quiet empty platforms, especially early morning and evening, I wonder if anyone today can envisage the scenes that I knew. In the morning traffic piled high on barrows on the platforms and in the office to await delivery; in the evening vans loading in the station yard, clerks and porters checking, weighing, stamping and again on to barrows through to the platforms to catch the evening trains.

All forwarded and received traffic (except fish) passed through the one big room for checking, charging, recording etc. Some of the "tools of the trade" where a large (very large) book "Classification of Merchandise", "Owner's Risk" and "Company's Risk" scales of charges, racks of stamps for charges raised (not self-adhesive — brush and glue pot required), consignment notes, delivery sheets etc. It should be remembered that in the days when there were large guard's vans and special parcels vans on passenger trains the size and weight of parcels (so called traffic) was considerable. Large firms forwarding regularly that I received were G. W. King (agricultural machine parts etc.), Herts & Beds Bacon Factory (large sides of bacon), Harkness Roses (small and large roses in straw wrapping), Samson of

Whitwell (watercress), Sharman Engineering and many smaller firms who could rely on the Railway for next day delivery over a wide area.

Above: the booking office at Hitchin Station, September 1955. (Ben Rawlings)

What else did we deal with? Amongst other things — motorcycles, cycles, perambulators, dogs on leads (with muzzles), cats, birds, mice in boxes, day-old chicks, pigeons in baskets (pigeons for special races and for local training flights) - not forgetting the horses by passenger train (in horse boxes of course!) A very popular facility was passenger luggage in advance - PLA - (anything from an attaché case to a cabin trunk) collected and delivered two shillings per package, delivered or collected, one shilling. I recall with feeling Princess Helena College start and end of term. Trunks arriving from all over the country — into the office, recorded and out for delivery. End of term, back into the office, checked, stamped (special PLA labels), back on to barrows, out to the trains. Worth a mention also are fruit and flowers which we received regularly. Local fruiterers could go on the early train to Covent Garden, where the Railway had a special receiving office, select the produce and it would be delivered at Hitchin before midday. Not bad for those "steam" days?

Our parcels van man in my time was Albert Andrews. Albert arrived at 8.30 a.m. to start loading. Incoming traffic had to be entered on to delivery sheets and stacked in readiness.

On most mornings the early turn parcels clerk (7 a.m. start) assisted by porters and often another clerk worked flat out to meet this deadline. I can recall on more than one occasion being unable to enter the office from the station yard at 7 a.m. and having to go round to the platform entrance and climb over piles of parcels to get to the desk and pencil and paper.

Incoming fish traffic was kept on the platform having arrived during the night from Hull, Grimsby, Peterhead, Mallaig and other places now probably long gone. Local fishmongers, particularly Mr Furr with a shop in Queen Street (and other Mr Furrs also in the fish business)[1] came early to collect their fish. Many local dignitaries had personal bags or boxes — Mr Delmé Radcliffe, Lord Lloyd of Offley, Mr Seebohm, Poynders End and others. On market day, Tuesday, Mr Wren of Biggleswade had fish delivered to Hitchin which he collected and took straight to market. Other market traders often arrived by train and took their cases by taxi to the market. Wren's fish stall is still here today!

The evening rush started around 5.30 p.m. when Albert arrived from the town with his first load. As time went on the larger firms such as G W King and the Bacon Factory bought in their own traffic. The clerk, with documentation, the porters with weighing machine and glue and brush were then hard at it working through the pile, each item to be checked against a consignment note, weighed, mileage to destination ascertained, charges calculated, stamps drawn and pasted on the package and barrows loaded on the platform to await the designated train. Two porters were needed to move the heavily loaded iron-wheeled barrows especially over the crossing at the north end of the platform, down the "downside" and up the "upside".

And in the quieter periods, for the clerks, there were cash books to be kept, correspondence, accounts to be prepared and various returns beloved by the Railway Management of those days.

On Sundays, one clerk only was on duty. He came on duty at around 6.30 a.m. and worked until 11 p.m., 16 ½ hours including ½hr for lunch (when I was on duty my mother, bless her heart, would send my father on his bicycle with a plate of hot dinner wrapped in a cloth). Sunday mornings in summer were especially busy with excursion trains to Skegness, Clacton, Yarmouth in addition to ordinary passengers.

Having worked hard all morning I was permitted to have my lunch and lock up the booking office for 2 hours. A kindly gesture by the management? Oh no — firstly I had to count my cash and balance my books from the morning — all by hand — no lovely machines that I see in there today. Then I collected from the safe 4 or 5 bags of money and cash books accumulated since Friday evening all to be amalgamated, entered into the register, cash counted and a balance struck (no difference permitted — possibly a ½ penny — subject to checking!) A cash note then made out and placed with the cash into a leather pouch, sealed

---

[1] Hence their nickname of "Fishy" Furr…

with the station seal and placed in the safe for the Chief Clerk to take to the designated train on Monday morning for the Cashier at Kings Cross.

I was not undisturbed! When the shutter on the small booking office window was closed the clerk was not visible from the booking hall. However, it was not unusual for persistent members of the public with enquiries to get a barrow under the barred windows facing the platform, hang on to the bars and shout from there! Sunday evenings were often lively. Many airmen changed at Hitchin after week-end leave to travel, to Henlow Camp on the old Hitchin — Bedford L. M. S. line. Trains from the north arrived on the "up" (to London) platform — the Henlow Camp train left from the "down" platform. Barriers were from time to time erected at the top of the subway on the "down" side for a special ticket check. This often yielded substantial revenue despite the ticket issues on the previous Friday, following the mass descent from Henlow Camp RAF. Airmen arrived in special coaches by road and a long queue quickly formed. From memory, many travelled north to stations for which we had no "printed stock." "Blank card" tickets had to be hand-written (outward and return). I can still recall the pressure — queues of people out into the station yard — find the destination, lookup the fare, write out the ticket, record in the "blank card" book, collect the cash and on to the next passenger. Failure to record the ticket was a disaster when time came to balance the books. After say, 2 hours solid booking the details were forgotten. The main hope was that blotting paper had been used and, with a mirror, some detail might be found. Another hope was to examine collected tickets later when the return half might be located.

All such booking activity particularly on weekdays was often undertaken with a steam engine waiting on the "down" platform, just outside the booking office. Making the noises beloved by enthusiasts but not so pleasant as a background to answering for example a detailed timetable enquiry. In fact I have known a train in the "down" platform, a train in the "up" platform and an engine taking on water on the down main line at the north end of the station, all together within ear splitting distance of the booking office. I learned to lip read early!

Mention of Mr Delmé Radcliffe earlier reminds me of a morning scene at Hitchin. The Station Master was often on the platform to lend importance to the prompt and efficient despatch of morning business trains to London and to greet the most important passengers. It was well known that the Priory clock was kept 5 minutes fast and on the occasions that Mr Delmé Radcliffe travelled his chauffeur departed for the station as the clock struck the hour. His train was I think, one or two minutes past the hour (L.N.E. Railway time) - he would arrive and pass through the booking hall with measured tread, glancing at his pocket watch as he did so, under the subway to the London platform. Whilst he didn't hurry I don't recall that he ever missed his train. I daresay that an ordinary passenger might have done so!

No longer a probationary clerk I was next moved to Knebworth to take duty, alone, on early and late turns. My opposite number lived at Knebworth and could take duty at say 5.45 a.m. — I could not since that was the first train from Hitchin. I was told that I should lodge at Knebworth on alternate weeks (station staff in the lower grades were moved around at the Company's discretion and it was not unusual for clerks having to deal with first and last trains to have to lodge (at their own expense!) However, I managed to argue that this would cause me undue hardship (true!) and I was permitted to arrive on the first train in the morning and, on alternate weeks, leave on the last train at night. This was achieved by the porter issuing any workman with a ticket for the first train (to London) and in the evening by me waiting with the booking office door ajar watching for the last "down" train to Hitchin ready to lock the door and rush up the steps to the platform praying that no-one would turn up for a ticket at the last minute!

There was a substantial service then on Christmas day and again I had to somehow get on an appropriate train to get home for Christmas dinner. After the War the service was gradually reduced and later cancelled altogether. I heard later that this occasioned a bitter complaint from a passenger who said that he visited his family at Knebworth regularly every Christmas day and cancellation of the 5.45a.m. train from Knebworth to London had caused him great inconvenience. A courteous reply was sent to the effect that whilst it was accepted that he had caught the train regularly, for several years he had been the only passenger and it was no longer economic to run the train!

From Knebworth I was called up to the Forces in 1940. The Railway Company paid me the balance of my salary until it was exceeded by my RAF pay. Although RAF pay was not generous it soon exceeded my railway salary. The rub came 5 ½ years later when returning to the Railway I was presented with a bill for the years of unpaid pension contributions. I found this hard to bear at the time but managed to pay by instalments and all these years later and long retired I am so glad that I did.

On returning from the Forces I was, after a time, placed on the Station relief staff, a small group of clerks who travelled around covering for sickness, annual leave and other staff shortages. Since we covered for staff who were usually on early and late turns of duty our hours were long and irregular but there were compensations. We could claim for travelling time and meal expenses and I was additionally fortunate in that my "home station" was Hitchin whereas I might have had to travel to, say, Hatfield or even Finsbury Park before I was officially "on duty" and eligible for additional payment. As even the smallest stations were open to the public from early morning until late at night continuous staffing was essential — I could be working at say Potters Bar in the morning and have a telephone call to go to Baldock at 2 o'clock to cover a clerk taken ill. Hard luck on the two or three staff at Potters Bar who, having been coping with staff shortage for weeks, had greeted me with joy but were now cast again into gloom!

The job was not without incident. Arriving by the first train at Enfield Chase one Monday morning there was an awful smell on the platform. Hurrying down below to the offices the cause was revealed — the parcels office contained a huge mound of bags of meat destined for a travelling circus that had lain there since Saturday evening. My first task was to despatch a porter, on his bicycle — fortunately a local man, to find the circus and bring someone back to take delivery with a message that otherwise we would have the meat condemned and removed by the local authority. Thankfully, he succeeded, and we gradually recovered.

Not long after this I was promoted to the London District Passenger Manager's Office (the section at the time (circa 1948/49) still evacuated to the L.N.E.R. sports ground at Gordon Hill (Enfield)). When we moved back to London (Liverpool Street) I entered another railway world and became a commuter. "Up" in the morning, "down" in the evening. I regret to say that I felt somewhat superior to those station clerks, on duty when I left, still there when I returned and with no respite on most Saturdays and Sundays! No going back — I had moved on!

Derrick Else
February 2000

Vol 12 no 3, September 2001

The Dell
Derek Wheeler
With acknowledgements to Ellie Clarke and Brian Sawford

In 1951 Hitchin held an historical Pageant. Whilst this was being planned, a more permanent memorial to that post-war go-ahead generation was being created. I of course refer to The Dell, situated as it is between Woodside car park and the flank of Windmill Hill.

My memories of this magic spot are a mixture of sheer trepidation, enjoyment and elation. As a child at Wilshere Dacre School in Coronation year I took part in a concert performed in the newly-opened Woodside Open Air Theatre. I was one of two boys singing in a choir of perhaps a hundred girls, under the baton of the fearsome Mrs Martin. She was a kindly soul under her strict exterior, but by golly, was she memorable! Later, as a teacher working with one of her former colleagues, Mr Pat Stokes, I was involved in the organisation of camping activities and sausage burning for the old HUDC's Play Scheme. This was pure fun just watching kids being kids in nature's own adventure playground!

The elation came many years later through being involved in one of Rosemary Bianchi's community plays, in this case, Hardy's *'Far From the Madding Crowd.'* The part of being a rustic yokel came easy to me, but being presented with a kit of hardboard farm cart bits on a

Saturday morning and being told to assemble it and make it run whilst carrying a coffin complete with (live) body was a challenge that most people would fear straight after breakfast! To be part of one of those productions in that setting was sheer elation. Long may our local dramatic societies in co-operation with NHDC keep this venue open!

Some early history

By 1844 the Dell and the hillside behind it were planted with trees. There was an excavation next to the Dell, and the Ordnance Survey map of 1881 shows a sand pit at the top of Windmill Hill. A document of 1644 refers to it as Rawlings Dell, and a map of 1770 shows it as 'a sand dell'. The 1818 Tithe Map has it as Rolling Dell, and it is described as 'waste'. Land around it is shown as owned by Mr Wilshere. The Tithe Map of 1844 names it as 'Rawlings Dell' with the tithe paid by Mr Wilshere.

By the 1880s ownership had passed to the Seebohm family. In 1880, Frederic Seebohm had a tunnel constructed under Walsworth Road to link his garden at the Hermitage to the Plantation opposite, called 'The Dell'.

When Frederic Seebohm died in 1912 the land passed to Esther, Margaret and Hilda Seebohm, and in 1928 they sold it to the Rev. George Bernard Gainsford.

The Inaugural performance at The Dell (Woodside Open Air Theatre) of 'A Midsummer Nights Dream' in 1951. (North Hertfordshire MuseumService)

In a will made in 1934, Elizabeth Constance Gainsford left Woodside and the land adjoining the garden known as 'The Dell' to her daughter Joan Cecily Allnutt. The will stipulated that on her death, the land was to go to the Elizabeth Gainsford Trustees, to be conveyed to Hitchin Urban District Council as a bird sanctuary in memory of Elizabeth's late husband, the Revd. Gainsford.

This appears to have been carried out prior to Joan Allnutt's death. On 15th August, 1939, the land was conveyed by Elizabeth Gainsford Trustees to Hitchin Urban District Council for use as a bird sanctuary, apparently with the stipulation that it not be used for any other purpose except with the consent of the Minister of Health. (Woodside car park is on the site of a house purchased by HUDC in 1939).

The central performing area of the open air theatre has been kept clear, and grassed, with a stone built stage. In the decades after its creation as an open-air theatre in 1951 it was used regularly for performances.[1]

The Dell has also become home to a considerable range of wildlife - tawny owls, great spotted woodpeckers, treecreepers, spotted flycatchers as well as the usual urban garden birds. Hedgehogs, bats and muntjac deer emerge after most of us have gone home. Snowdrops carpet its perimeter in late winter, as do bluebells in spring and dog-rose in summer. Butterflies and, increasingly, dragonflies are evident, but this idyll has not always been so.

The Dell Enhancement Project

Through the 1980s and early 1990s The Dell was neglected and vandalised. It consequently became increasingly difficult to hold public events, there being so much broken glass and rubbish. During Hitchin Festival's Teddy Bears' Picnic in July 1994, two children were cut by broken glass. The Dell was closed to public use for health and safety reasons.

Working with Groundwork Hertfordshire, Countryside Management Service and NHDC who between them provided expert advice and funding, Hitchin Forum began a staged programme of improvements using local volunteers.

During 1994/95 several massive clean-ups were undertaken by volunteers in organised working parties. The aim was to make the place safe and more inviting for dog walkers and those just strolling. The Forum liaised with the police to report anything untoward, and a team of local residents undertook to clear the rubbish weekly.

In. July 1995, following a public consultation undertaken by Groundwork Hertfordshire, wooden steps and railings were installed by volunteers from Hitchin Forum and Countryside Management Service, with professional help from Groundwork, and funding from the

---

[1] When I was a boy at Wilshere-Dacre School in the 1950s I went to see a performance of *A Midsummer Night's Dream*. My abiding recollection is not so much the play as the mosquitos! [SLW]

District Council and the Department of the Environment. This greatly improved The Dell, both visually and in terms of access for those with limited mobility.

By October 1995 improvements were sufficient to enable the Council to reopen The Dell to public use. It was inaugurated with a spectacular performance of *Beowulf* by drama students at North Herts College.

Right: The sign board at the entrance to the Dell.

In 1996 further improvement work was undertaken with stage repairs and tree planting. In early 1997 Hitchin Forum volunteers planted 75 trees provided by Groundwork along the perimeter fence to improve its appearance. Later that year the Forum surveyed the entire perimeter area to assess how The Dell could be made more inviting and accessible. They approached the Council to remove the barbed wire along the top of the perimeter fence and create new gates to improve the external appearance of The Dell. The Council funded and carried out all these works.

In 1998, with financial support from the District and County Councils, Countryside Management Service and Hitchin Forum, a sign-board was produced and set into a tree stump at the entrance to The Dell. It tells a little of the history and environment of The Dell and invites people to enjoy themselves in this wonderful open-air amphitheatre. The Dell is a magical place to be in the waking light of dawn, as light and sound recede at dusk, in the dappled sunlight of a late summer afternoon, and in the crisp moonlight after a fresh snowfall. People and wildlife cohabit its environs in happy harmony. Long may that be!

Russell's Slip[1] or 'The Slype'
The origin of the name
by Aud Eastham

When I was researching the street names of Hitchin for the series of books recently published,[2] I asked somebody who had been a Hitchin resident much longer than I have, whether he knew anything about the names Russell's Slip and Maxwell's Path. I was told that "Nobody knows", and that I was unlikely to be able to find out . . . I remember being somewhat disheartened and wondering why I had agreed to take on this task. It may still be true that nobody knows for certain but I began to gather together my information and this brief article is a summary of the facts and theories I developed on the way and the conclusions I reached.

The definition of 'slip' or 'slype' is a narrow strip of land, which indeed it is. The proprietor and tenant of the whole strip appears to have been Mr. Thomas Jeeves. In 1820, it was shown as enclosed by a hedge with no buildings on it and even at this early date it was known as Russell's Slip. In 1832, William Lucas referred to it when he said, "the pleasant piece of greensward called Russells Slipe was being developed." It is most likely that the earliest houses were built by one of the Jeeves family, probably James Cawdell Jeeves. Later on, George Jeeves was reprimanded by the Local Board for building without the required permission and could not proceed until his plans were approved. The 1851 0.S. map refers to it as Russell's Slite or Russellslite but this may only be a mis-transcription.

In May 1857 the Inspector of Nuisances recommended the use of tar on a footpath for the first time, which the Gas Company had given him free of charge. The path in question was Russell's Slip. In 1877, the Superintendent of Roads, Mr. George Farrer, reported a stoppage in the main sewer in the area of Russell's Slipe, which it took four men six days to unblock along a length of three hundred yards. Mr. Farrer attributed it to the smallness of the pipes, which were a mere six inches in diameter. There were then twenty cottages using the drain.

The Medical Officer of Health reported fever in the cottages in 1884 and there were complaints that pigs were being kept in the Slipe. Scarlet Fever reared its ugly head in 1888.

When James Foster died in 1860, his widow Eliza sold the Wheelwright's business to her brother-in-law and moved from Park Street to 6, Russell's Slip. Numbers 5, 6 and 7 are now all one house and Mr. and Mrs. Radmall confirm that these cottages and Number 8 were once in the ownership of the Fosters and were built in about 1840.

---

[1] Russell, or Russell's, Slip runs as a footpath starting beside the Highlander in Upper Tilehouse Street to Wratten Road, which it crosses; from there it runs parallel to Meadow Way, and then on to Hawthorn Close.

[2] *The Street Names of Hitchin*, three volumes, Hitchin Historical Society.

However, when Henry Jeeves died in 1920, Numbers la, 2, 3, 4, 6 and 7 were owned by Henry Jeeves' Trustees and rented out. John Shilcock conducted an auction and it seems that the Foster family acquired some of the cottages from the Jeeves family at this time. So although James Jeeves died, still a young man, his family was well provided for by virtue of the rents of these cottages.

The name, Russell's Slipe appears very early in the nineteenth century - too early to refer to the leather tanners who came to Hitchin from Isleworth in Middlesex. At one stage I wondered whether the name was a reference to Lord John Russell, the Liberal M.P. for Bedfordshire who perhaps came into Hitchin from this direction, or whether it referred to Isaac or John Russell who were Bootmakers in the Churchyard at the turn of the eighteenth century.

Finally, I decided that the most likely candidate for the naming of Russell's Slip is Edward Russell who was a gardener in 1793. At this time gardeners were also called greengrocers. Edward Russell was one such and a freeholder who in 1776 was designated a Highlander. This may indicate that he was a Scot since some think Russell is a Scottish name, or it may be that he was settled or worked close by the Highlander, for instance, in Russell's Slipe.

Interestingly, Edward Russell was Master of the Workhouse from 1778 to 1784. This was the Workhouse which stood in Tilehouse Street near to the Priory entrance before its removal to Bancroft and after that, to Chalkdell in 1837.

Vol 12 no 4, March 2002

The Churchyard - Sport and Leather Activities
by Derek Wheeler

There are some shop interiors that stay in the memory from childhood and never fade. A suddenly savoured can trigger distant associations with people and places long vanished. The smell of new leather always reminds me of holiday work done as a teenager in D. F. Jackson's shop which fronted High Street at the bottom of Brand Street and continued rearwards into the Churchyard. One can still enter the premises but it is but a shadow of its former self.

How I came to spend six Saturdays working in this interesting shop in the early 1960's still amazes me, since my credentials for applying for the job were non-existent. Anyone who went to Hitchin Boys' Grammar School was expected to be a sportsman; you were not considered to be a fully rounded person if you could not catch a fully rounded ball, or in the case of rugby, a somewhat deformed ball. [1]

---

[1] *I have a lot of sympathy with Derek on this – I went through similar treatment. I still flinch at the thought of cricket balls flying towards me, hoping I'd be able to get out of their way… SLW*

Above: Hitchin Boys' Grammar School in the early 20th century. This view was not much changed when Derek was at the school. (SLW)

The English master, Smiler Miles, would relate about his games prowess at Oxford and end a lesson with the poem 'Vitae Lampada' which contains the famous line 'Play up and play the game…..' well, I didn't want to play any game, and so I wasn't a fully rounded person. Having said that, some of my contemporaries who did play the game are now so fully rounded that they can no longer play any game, but I digress.

Gym lessons for the non-muscular eleven-year-old meant a quarter-mile sprint from the North Court to the old town gymnasium behind the Town Hall at 2.15 every Monday and Wednesday afternoon. If your white shorts and white shoes were not of that colour or creased in the wrong places you were slippered by a row of grinning teeth surmounting a dimpled chin answering to the name of Basher Bartlett. If you were the last one changed you were slippered and if you were the last one back in the French class at 2.55 you had to brace yourself for the sadistic lash of Bert Reid's tongue. He could command silence by just a look but he had an enlightened attitude to games; he regarded card playing as strenuous physical activity and only just about tolerated chess.

Games to me either meant the lash, one way or the other, or it meant getting wet, cold, or dirty sometimes all three at once. Getting wet is all right if you are going from A to B for a purpose, likewise for getting cold. Getting dirty is acceptable if you are making, mending,

105

growing or finding something. To suffer all three in the pursuit of an inanimate object, such as a ball, with the possibility of suffering broken bones was to me a mugs game. Wet games days were prayed for in my home, both summer and winter; gas leaks, outbreaks of bubonic plague in the staff room or an influx of itinerant musicians all jockeyed for first place in my fantasy prayer book. Where I really wanted to be was:-

   a) in the library
   b) doing my homework in school time
   c) in the art room/workshop

As you can see I was hardly the material to be working in a sports shop selling sporty goods to sporty people and knowing about as much about the noble art of whatever as the pseudo aesthete who thought a pas-de-deux was a father of twins.

Whilst my contemporaries were developing their character by kicking balls into touch, wherever that might be, I was honing my creative skills in the garden shed or kitchen table (on cold days) and this penchant for making do and mend gave me plenty of pocket money which came from many grateful sources. I did not need to find extra income to support youthful riotous living, since having a home-made lathe in the kitchen was living dangerously enough for me. However a sixth-form friend of mine who later became a professional graphic artist wanted to leave his weekend and holiday job at Jackson's to do some landscape painting and photography before going to art college. He said that as his best mate, I was in line to take over his job at Jackson's. He told me it was only for six Saturdays, 8.30am until 5.30pm July and August.

I must have protested feebly but found myself earning real money in a shop run by real characters. The manager, a gentle avuncular man named Mr Bygrave was warmly welcoming, ever patient and genuinely interested in people. In my youthful imagination I could see him going home to pipe and slippers, soggy spaniel and acres of immaculately kept lawn. I believe he was the ageing Mrs. Jackson's son-in-law but I never met her. He knew leather and harness, martingales and niblicks[1] and other words I do not understand, but above all, like all good tradesmen, he knew his customers and the names of their children and of course, the customers always came back, because it was a traditional family firm where service mattered.

I often had to go aloft in this quaint shop, which meant climbing two flights of narrow stairs to an attic of Dickensian obsolescence. Seated here was a lovely elderly lady with the characterful name of Ethel Ramsbottom. She handled the day-today book-keeping, using

---

[1] [*Martingale*: a word with a number of definitions. Here it means a strap or set of straps running from the noseband or reins to the girth of a horse to prevent the horse from raising its head too high." It can also be part of the rigging of a sailing vessel's bowsprit, attached to the dolphin striker, referred as the "martingale stay." There are others. A *niblick* is a type of golf club. SLW]

wooden in and out trays and fearsome metal spikes upon which she hung invoices. She would decant change from canvas bags, some containing pennies, others three-penny bits and others half-crowns which, of course weighed a great deal in those pre-decimal coinage days. I often wondered how she knew about so many people and what was going on in the town, since she used to be so isolated in this antique crow's nest of an office, but I later realised that she used to sit by an open window above the Churchyard in summer and could hear all that was said below her and could watch people's comings and goings without herself being noticed!

If she sat surrounded by the ledgers and tiles of essentially an Edwardian business, she sat next to an even more intriguing attic. This wondrous glory hole had once been the nerve centre of the whole business, for this abandoned eyrie was where the craft of saddlery had been practised long before short sojourn at Jackson's. Here, covered in cobwebs, were saddles, bridles, riding crops, wicker receptacles for parasols on dog carts, straps of all descriptions and wondrously-smelling hides, just waiting for the skilled tooling of a first-class craftsman. This was a timewarp. There was a post horn in there, just as though Mr. Kershaw's guard had just gone out for a smoke whilst awaiting a new set of reins for his master! There were ice skates there, of the type my father had purchased as a boy to skate on Lax's pond at St. Ippolyts at the end of World War 1. There were tennis rackets awaiting restringing of a type Victorian ladies carried in Latchmore photographs.

As one climbed the stairs there were tins of products which were long past their sell-by date: saddle soap, blacking, hoof oil and 'Chemico' motorists' soap, the motorist on the faded yellow tin wearing a polar bear skin overcoat and goggles. He had just been greasing the chains on his Panhard-Levassor car, no doubt. Mr Bygrave wouldn't sell me some of these tins, he gave them to me and I used this volcanic lava-and-treacle mixture for years on my hands and it was quite remarkable in its power to remove everything... including the skin!

On the first floor, in a room facing Brand Street, was where my powers of invention and downright lying came into their own. This is where I spent hours of abject boredom, punctuated by the odd welcome tea break, by trying to sell football boots to people who had really come in to complain about how badly Arsenal were doing this year. Until then I had always associated Arsenal with Woolwich and big guns but I soon came to understand that they were some kind of mass event that people paid good money to complain about. One of the good things about dishing out football boots and footballs was that they sometimes inadvertently necessitated a big adventure for me.

Jackson's like other shops of the time, had large sun blinds, surmounted by the legend 'Deans of Putney which' came down across the shop frontage. Mr. Bygrave used to hang up footballs in nets from these blinds, or rather, Mrs. Kitching, who was rather taller than all of us, used to hang them up. Yobbos used to remove them when the shop was busy on a Saturday, Mr. B used to report them missing and I had to go down to the old police station and give a description of a missing football, which-I-hadn't-seen-officer-'cos-I-was-selling-footballs-at-the-time. Occasionally a well-meaning passer-by would give chase and a hotly-pursued string bag with-or-without contents would turn up in the nick. I would then have to say this was one of Jackson's footballs which-I-hadn't-witnessed-at-the-time-'cos-I-was-too-busy-selling footballs.

For generations there had been a diminutive lady named Mrs. Weeden working in Jackson's. She was a widow I believe but was a mother to all of us. She used to make the tea and keep Mr. Bygrave busy whilst allowing me to investigate hidden yet infinitely interesting corners of the shop. She would send me into the rear cellar, which adjoined Churchyard, simply because she knew I was curious about what was down there... medieval bricks, dampness and old cabin trunks, the sort P&O travellers used to let other people lug around. Is that why we call it 'luggage'? I've often wondered! She used to send me on excursions up to West Hill to see Bert Wells in his wonderful 1919 garage.

Above: Wells' Garage in the 1960s, looking much as it would have done in Derek's day. (Pansy Mitchell)

In those far-off days, football boots used to have studs which screwed in to the sole; they may still do, for all I know, but that's another matter. Anyway, when the screwed shank snapped or performed another alliterative process, the only answer to the problem was to go and see Bert. He kept a special stud extractor for the purpose and sent me back to screw in another stud. With hindsight, why didn't Jackson's keep a stud extractor themselves?

One trip I never went on, although I dropped enough heavy hints, was a trip into the front cellar, facing High Street. I was told it was smelly because it often flooded. There was a tantalising trap door in the shop floor with a brass ring in it just waiting to be lifted, but I never did. What mysteries does that cellar hold and what mysteries do other old premises adjoining Churchyard conceal? If you know, please let us into your confidence!

The shop is long gone and leaves a gap in the market for some enterprising tradesman. We still occasionally need leather straps, not necessarily in a standard plasticised length; we still need a sympathetic repair to a piece of sports kit: we still need a wheel to be replaced on a heavy suit case and we shouldn't have to travel miles to equip our daughters with jodhpurs or riding hats. Come back the likes of D.F. Jackson of Churchyard and High Street!

Right: This advertisement is interesting to a local historian, since the information it contains enables one to go to the old census returns or town directories and find out who occupied the premises way back in the 19th century. I know that a saddler named Paddon, who doubled as a schoolmaster, ran the business until Raban took over, but who preceded Paddon? Perhaps the answer lies below that front cellar trapdoor! (D Wheeler)

Hitchin Thespians – a Century of Success

Derek Wheeler

In the last Journal I noted that our lovely Town Hall was now a century old. A local organisation whose early days are inextricably linked with the 'Old Lady of Brand Street' is the Hitchin Thespians.

The origins of the Thespians go back to a little-publicised performance by an all-ladies cast of Coleridge-Taylor's 'The Gitanos.' The show was organised by Mrs Walter Carling and Miss Cane. It was such a success that the Rev. G. B. Gainsford, Vicar of St. Saviour's Church, convened a meeting at his house 'Birchfield' in Verulam Road on 21st February, 1903, with the object of forming a group of likeminded people to be subsequently called 'The Hitchin Amateur Light Opera Company'. Those present included the Vicar and Mrs Gainsford, Mr and Mrs R. C. Swaine, Miss Pepper and Miss Cane. They constituted the first Committee.

The first performance was of Gilbert and Sullivan's *'The Sorcerer'* on the 10th February 1904. With odd departures from a successful pattern, G. and S. was the standard fare until the late 1920s.

One of the drawbacks of the early performances was the heat generated by the gas footlights. Mr P. A. Sharman made a test with a thermometer and the mercury broke the glass on stage! The Hitchin Electric Supply Corporation responded to pleas to the Council and electric stage lights were installed in 1906, but the auditorium still had its gas lighting. If you look carefully in the right place in the Town Hall you can still see where the gas pipes were later blanked off.

My earliest recollections of Thespians productions go back to the late 1940's and early 1950's when my mother would take me on a Saturday afternoon once a year, down the dark subterranean passage which contained all the queues for the Hermitage Cinema. Shuffling along down a damp ramp which would eventually turn back on itself, rise and lead the Hitchin film goers into the carpeted opulence of the 'Herm' foyer. Thespians regulars would collect their tickets and go into the stalls or rise up the dimly-lit staircase to the balcony restaurant where the nostrils were tantalised by the alternate aromas of disinfectant and coffee.

On this once-a-year pilgrimage, we would settle in the second tier of the balcony, where the regulars would pay 2s 7d for a cinema seat. The front row 'three and nines' were 'far too extravagant' for my mother to 'fork out for.'

Once settled, my infant mind would grasp the wonder of the dim interior, the tiny lights in the ceiling looking like so many stars trapped in ice cream tubs, the twin classical urns, one each side of the auditorium, casting its mellow glow upwards. And the magic expectation engendered by the footlights' glare upon the faded brown of the curtains.

Filmgoers made heroes and heroines of the stars. I only had one Thespians hero. He would always be, not on stage, but in the orchestra pit. This hero was Charlie Pettengell: by day he was a plumber or builder working for French's in Whinbush Road, pushing a barrow with ladders or buckets on. On one special afternoon in the year he would crash his cymbals and bang his drums so skilfully, that I wanted to sit in that pit one day myself and be Charlie Pettengell! I can never hear *'Tokay'* from the 1951 Noel Coward Thespians production of 'Bitter Sweet' without seeing Charlie in my mind, his brass cymbal dangling from its budgie cage stand. Here's to the next century of Thespians shows!

Whilst we are congratulating the Thespians on their magnificent centenary, we must also thank them for their evening of magic and nostalgia at the Hitchin Historical Society's Christmas Party. It is so refreshing to be entertained by live performers in familiar surroundings. I know what a wonderful evening the members enjoyed!

Whilst we are still thinking about the Thespians, what about their clever advertising technique in their 1926 souvenir programme? The programme, for a joint performance of *'Trial by Jury'* and *'H.M.S. Pinafore,'* and what better way to enliven someone else's advertising material than by advertising your own past successes (see below). As the late Leonard Sachs in the 'Good Old Days Music Hall' might have said, "I give you not only Mr Leslie Rands as Sir Marmaduke Pointdextre, but also your own, your very own, Mr C. C. Blundell as Robin Oakapple, fresh from the haze of a tobacco ad."

Left: an advertisement for Merrick Bros, next to the Arcade. In these days the line, "FOR EVERYTHING YOU SMOKE" might raise an eyebrow. The 1920s was a less cynical age.

Shopping in Hitchin Fifty Years Ago
by Brian Worbey

The opening in September of the large new Sainsbury's Supermarket made me think of when Hitchin's first supermarket (Keymarket in Churchgate) opened in the mid-1970s and how our shopping has changed in the town in the last fifty years.

Back in the early 1950s Hitchin was a town of about 19,000 people. We had a church in St John's Road. The Angel Pub was still in Sun Street and the Oakfield Estate was still being planned. Housing on Rosehill or Poets Corner was not even thought about!

We had a cattle, pig and sheep market and even with the large market on St Mary's Square the town had seventeen greengrocers, yes seventeen!

These included:

Fred Worbey	Bob Gates
Watson's	Mrs A Day
Wheelers	Gordon Day
Upchurch	Croxton's
Tomlin	Cannon's
Rainbow	Brown's
John Howard	Albone
Elizabeth Howard	Abbiss Brothers
Halsey's	

Well done to John Webb in the Churchyard, the last dedicated greengrocer in town!

The 1950s was still the day of the corner shop but the town centre still had a number of grocers. As you walked up Bancroft from Blake's Corner we started with David Greig's, C H Payne then on to shop at Moss's, into the High Street - Greig's again - the Market Place with the Maypole, Home & Colonial. Bucklersbury had the International and Stowell's, into Churchyard with Halsey's and Halsey's and Harry's Store in Arcade Walk and also the Sun Stores at 24 Sun Street. Finally there was Haysom's in Hermitage Road.

No national ladies outfitters like Mackays, Dorothy Perkins or Next could be found in Hitchin fifty years ago but the fair sex were well served with fifteen shops and of those P A Smith had four - in Bancroft, Hermitage Road and Arcade Walk.

Gentlemen's tailors were also well to the fore with around seventeen shops. In Bucklersbury alone you had the choice of Waldocks, Leete, Powells and Hawkins.

On the food side, with regard to butchers you could find eighteen around the town and fish was also on the menu for you had the choice of eight fishmongers as well as a wholesale fishmonger, Stirk Brothers, in West Alley.

The town still misses the old fashioned department stores such as Spurr's and Nicholls, those were the days!

I could go on, but getting back to 2002 we all hope the Churchgate problems are quickly resolved to keep Hitchin as a major shopping centre.

It is good that the old names like Bliss, Burgess Books, Woodbridge, Brookers, Hawkins, Allinghams, Halseys, Pomfrets, Philpotts, Gatwards etc. are still with us fifty years on. *[Some of these shops are still here; sadly though, some are not. SLW]*

Vol 12 no 4, March 2002

The Sainsbury's Legacy

A. B. Eastham

Early in 1970 there were rumours that a Sainsbury's store was coming to Hitchin and a little later that year the 'Dog' public house closed its doors for the last time. As the weeks went by, it became apparent that the intended site for the store in Brand Street entailed the demolition of the 'Dog' public house, the Brand Street Methodist Church and the garage of H. A. Saunders.

Above: The Dog, Brand Street. Left, H. A. Saunders, next to the Methodist church. (SLW)

During the demolition of the Methodist Church, two coffins were discovered underneath it, and a silver birch tree, at least five years old, was removed from the roof and planted in the grounds of the new Christchurch building. The coffins were believed to contain the remains of a childless couple who founded the church, Thomas and Sophia Ward. Their Manse was known as Chesham House and the main burial ground lay on the opposite side of the road. The church had been built in 1834, which was also the time when Pound Lane was opened up to become Brand Street, after Thomas Brand,[1] and when William Jeeves' widow removed from Cock Street [now the High Street] to Queen Street, her house, lying as it did, in the way of the widening. It seems that 1834 brought as much change as did the 1970s.

In December 1971, the Hitchin Society declared war on the plans for the Sainsbury's Supermarket. It was also fighting plans for a spur road entailing; a dual carriageway from Mann Egerton's Garage in Queen Street to Letchworth.[2] The prime mover in this fight was Miss Mary Aughton, who organised a petition which not only prevented the building of the road, but also preserved the three step-terraced houses built by George Jeeves opposite the British Schools. However, the plans for the new Sainsbury's store were ready in January of 1972 and scraped past the approval panel in April.

It had been decided that the Sainsbury's design could include a mural capturing significant events in the history of Hitchin. By September of that year the mural had been designed in collaboration with Miss Mary Gadd, the Curator of Hitchin Museum, and it was duly passed by Mr Martin Priestman, the Consultant Architect for the Council, and by the County Planning Officer.

The mural was the joint effort of a husband and wife called Henry and Joyce Collins of Colchester. It was so large that it had to be made in sections. Their method of working was described as follows by a reporter of the time:-

"Joyce and Henry start off with a working drawing of the complete mural. Each panel is then re-drawn full-size on tracing paper and the images are transferred on to a sheet of expanded polystyrene by pricking it with a sharp pen. The polystyrene is cut with implements similar to spoons, pastry cutters, spanners and bits of metal, which are heated upon the Collins' gas-stove and used to melt the polystyrene. The fine work is done with copper nibs which Henry makes and attaches to a soldering iron. When the polystyrene moulds are complete, they are taken to a local builder's yard to be filled with a special concrete mix."

The work went ahead and was almost ready when disaster struck in August 1973. Two pieces of the huge mural were broken and had to be remade. They were set in place just

---

[1] One of the MPs for Hertfordshire at the time.
[2] There was a protest about the dual carriageway, as it involved biting into Windmill Hill to build a roundabout at the top of Hermitage Road. I was part of the protest! SLW

over a fortnight later than scheduled. The new Sainsbury's shop in Hitchin was the third store in the country to receive such a mural. One had been erected on the site of the Colchester store, because the use of glass was restricted in the planning there.

The Hitchin mural, which depicted the town's history by displaying various animals, ploughs and haycarts, was set in place by three men using a forklift truck. It was very heavy work with some of the pieces weighing as much as a hundredweight each.

The new Sainsbury's store, which cost in the region of one and a quarter million pounds, opened in August 1973. It has now been superseded by another new store in Bancroft, which opened belatedly in 2001 on the site of Russell's Tannery.

Above: the Sainsbury's mural. At the instigation of Hitchin Historical Society, the mural was later moved to Hitchin Library, where it remains to this day. The meaning of many of the panels is clear; others less so. (SLW)

Bibliography:
Herts. Pictorial

Volume 13 no 1, October 2002

Reflections on Hitchin Carnival

Derek Wheeler

I am very sad to see the demise of Hitchin's annual Carnival. As a teenager I was at the grass roots of its foundation. The story begins in 1962.

While I was studying for my `A' Levels a group of a similarly-aged young people, calling themselves `The Local Yokels' frequented such dens of iniquity as the 'Red Hart' yard and the nurses' quarters at the old Lister Hospital. Led by a sport-loving member of the staff at Letchworth, John Harrison, this small core of enthusiastic drinkers voted to put all their energy during the dismal winter months into organising a carnival for Hitchin and

Letchworth. The ultimate aim was to raise funds for the League of Friends of the North Herts Hospitals. As a successful result of their efforts, armchairs, televisions and other comforting luxuries began to enliven the otherwise stark wards at the old hospitals.

Silly things were organised for us all to do on Saturday mornings prior to Carnival Day. One of my near neighbours in Nightingale Road was Brian Furr, of the Hitchin fishmongering family. He had an ancient Austin Seven as everyday transport which we used to decorate with posters and placards. I had just found and restored a 1907 James pedal tricycle which I had started to ride around the district for fun... Brian and his friend Brian Piggott saw me in Bedford Road and uttered the immortal words, "You must be one of us and if you're not, then you are now."

From then on I was a Local Yokel, out on Saturdays in strange costume, pedalling furiously whilst carrying a placard on the back of the trike and handing out flyers to all and sundry. There was I, sitting on a kerbstone in Brand Street, dangling a fishing line through a drain grating, with one of the Furr's best bloaters on the end of the hook. A group of about twenty people (and I believe at one time our worthy `Comet' photographer, Alan Millard, took part in these activities) performed the Yokels' version of Rag Day stunts.

There was always a Carnival Queen competition at the old Hermitage Halls or the Town Hall, a Carnival Queen Ball and various pram races around and into the pubs of Hitchin. Very unusual babies would be pushed at break-neck speed in customised prams, pushchairs, wheelchairs and wheelbarrows through the streets and a great deal of ale was consumed at the various stopping places. Hospital beds took to the streets and chamber pots assumed a new function as ever more of the magic brews were imbibed.

We took part in other towns' carnivals, advertising our own. The trike and other old bicycles went to Biggleswade, to St. Neots and also to Stevenage, in our ever-increasing advertising campaign to spread awareness of the work of the League of Hospital Friends. A group of us even spent best part of a day going by train and coach to Maldon in Essex to take part in their carnival.

I reflected that whilst I was pedalling and steaming along the summer carnival routes, my father had coaxed an asthmatic Ford `Model T' lorry around the pre-war Hitchin carnivals, with its low gear crying out for mercy and its radiator boiling all the way, the very same Ford that had rejected the bite of its own handbrake and nearly consigned my mother to a watery grave in the watercress beds at Whitwell, but I digress!

These 1960s carnivals introduced me to a local man of steam, the late Brian Halley, of Great Wymondley. His neighbours were the Pinkstone family and Jill Pinkstone was the Yokels' Secretary. Many summer events happened in Brian's barn, with his magnificent traction engines as a feature. It came to pass that a young teacher would discard the bikes and get into steam and follow the engines to rallies. The rest, as they say, is history.

By courtesy of the Hertfordshire Express, 1963:

by JOHN QUILL:

A NUMBER of North Hertfordshire young people went daft for the day on Saturday in the most amiable and admirable sort of way. And I for one hasten to congratulate the Local Yokels on their carnival revival.

First of all it gives the lie to those who say that young people do nothing but hang about on street corners and get into trouble - these didn't. They met and talked and worked for 18 months to bring their plans to fruition.

And it's not just the hospitals that will benefit from their money-raising. For isn't it a change to see a whole town turn out in a spirit of happy friendship chatting with perfect strangers along the - route, inhibitions left at home for the afternoon?

A pity that more shopkeepers didn't put out decorations - those who did showed the right idea. In view of the success of the procession probably many more will climb on the carnival bandwagon next year.

Another good point—Letchworth and Hitchin were joined by this Jolly event. A sense of friendly rivalry between the two neighbouring towns is a healthy thing: but haughty isolation is not good for either of them. In the carnival they shared the hard work in advance and shared the general jollification on Saturday.

Well, there was some traffic dislocation. Some cars were held up, others had to slow down and take diversionary routes. Tut tut, what a pity.

It wasn't for long and it wasn't all that tragic. And it didn't count very much against all the fun and games that people were able to have as a result of the carnival. It was a tonic. a shot in the arm, and it put the motor car in its proper place as the community's servant and not its master.

There's only one really apt comment on the whole affair to address to the Local Yokels - Jolly good show - and do it again.

Right: a spoof advertisement from 1963.

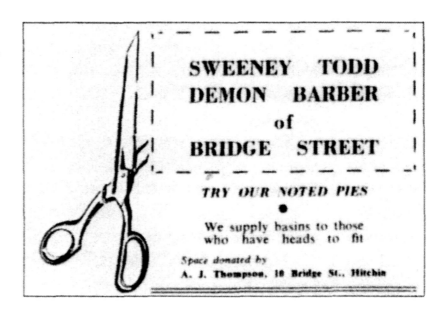

Volume 13 no 1, October 2002

Well, Well: a Newly Found Well in the Hitchin British School Old Playground

Dr John Horton

As recent rescue archaeology has amply shown in Hitchin over the past 2 years, what is hidden is not necessarily uninteresting or unimportant, and can reveal evidence of activities of our forebears. Experience has shown that some of the most enduring and interesting evidence of the past comes from domestic activity, cooking pots and fires, middens, and water supplies. The latter, especially if it is a well, can survive for a very long time even with complete destruction of all other domestic structures around it.

Water is, of course, very important, and in medieval castles, a secure supply was needed to survive a siege. However, the same was also true for the humble cottar — no water, no life. Hence, towns like Hitchin were established close to an abundant water supply. As towns expanded, wells both small and large were dug down into the water table to supply the increasing need. An easy task if you are close to the river, but much of Hitchin is built on the steep slope of the Chiltern escarpment, and so, the further away from the river and up the hill you go, the deeper the well must be. Three wells were identified during the construction of the Jeeves' Yard development, and now another has come to light higher up the hill.

A few weeks back, prior to the start of the new development above Storehouse Lane, a well was accidentally unearthed, It is assumed that a mechanical digger doing preliminary work disturbed the capping stone of a deep well under the old playground of Hitchin British Schools.

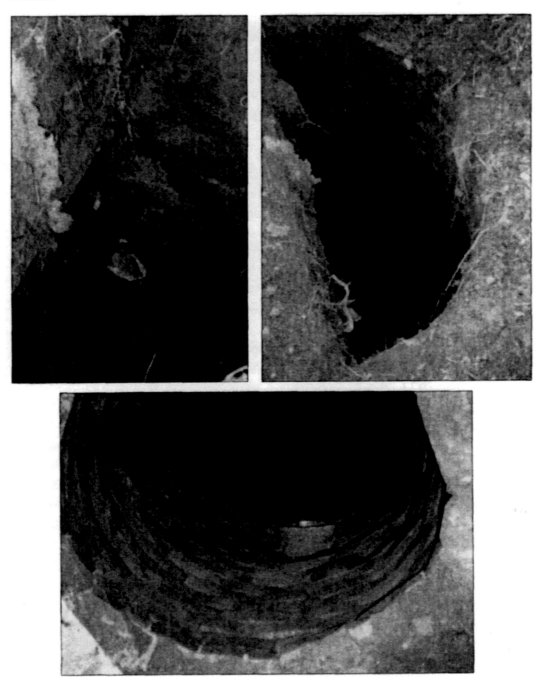

Above: Three views of the well in Hitchin British Schools old playground (courtesy Dr John Horton)

One capping stone fell to the bottom, some 20 - 30 feet down, onto other debris from the past. The bottom is dry, as the infill is now above the water table. It is perhaps lucky that the capstones were substantial; otherwise there might be a record of a child playing at school vanishing from sight.

The question is why was there a well there in the first place? There are no records of any dwellings on the site, and none of the 19th century maps suggests either buildings or a well being there. The map evidence shows that in 1820, the area was in open fields and the fields where the cemetery is now situated even show medieval open field plough patterns.

By the 1890s, a nursery or market garden is marked on the map, with, if Ordnance Survey symbols have not changed, a substantial set of greenhouses half way up the hill. No well is marked on either the 1851 or 1898 Hitchin map, and it is unlikely that the surveyors would have missed out such a substantial feature, even in a town.

Furthermore, there is no record in the Public Health maps of the late 19th century. A secure water supply would have been needed on the rather dry slope to supply the water needs of the nursery, and presumably the well was dug sometime around 1900 to provide such a source. By 1923, the greenhouses had vanished, and the area of the school playground is apparent while, at one corner, there is a tiny building. This is very close to where the well was found, and it is likely that this was a building to house the well head equipment.

Examination of the brickwork and mortaring, which extends all the way to the visible base, suggests that it is probably late Victorian or early Edwardian in construction. The appearance is also similar to the well at the top of the Jeeves' Yard development, which would have a similar construction date based on building patterns. There is no obvious clue at present as to how the water was obtained, but there is a metal beam across the mouth (at 1.5 metres diameter, this was not a small well), and this could suggest a hand or mechanical pump (perhaps driven by a small gas engine) being used rather than the traditional bucket and rope. It is to be hoped that some investigation of the depths will be possible before the well is finally sealed and built over.

A final intriguing question comes from further up the site. Another `collapsed' area was reported at the same time as the well was identified, and although superficial investigation does not suggest this is another well, it is positioned at one end of where the old greenhouses (and a small extension to them) are marked on maps. While excavation of this site would probably provide the answer, the position and size is consistent with this being the boiler house for heating the Victorian greenhouses.

Victorian Pubs in Hitchin

Derek Wheeler

The following ditty was written by George Albert Burrows in 1867 as a song. Unfortunately we do not have the music. The words were found in the Museum archives and I must apologise if they have appeared before in this *Journal*. He knew where all the pubs were!

In the days before universal literacy was assumed, pub signs were valuable direction markers, especially for lost travellers, and this was true right across Europe. They knew no language barriers.

If the French should invade us or ever be inclined,
The Landlords of Hitchin have made up their minds
That if Napoleon the III should dare to draw near
The Tyrant they will drown in Three Tuns *of small beer.*
At the sign of the Angel *the coward will shrink*
And from the Red Cow *he will get nothing to drink.*
From the Highlander *brave he will speedily flee*
And the Trooper *will frighten him into the sea.*
The King's Head *and* Queen's *will together unite,*
And in defence of the Crown *most bravely will fight.*
From the Swan *and the* Cock *he will hook it and run*
And the Post Boy *and* Jockey *will at him poke fun.*
The White *and* Red Lions *will for freedom still fight,*
And Adam and Eve *crack their sides with delight,*
To see Boney the III and his arms go to pot,
And I am sure he'll confess that the Sun *is too hot.*
The Black *and* White Horses *will him disaster,*
And the French Eagle *will find the* Falcon *his master.*
The Two Brewers *will fight in defence of the Town,*
And the Red Hart *will run crafty Boney to the ground.*
Though the Wheatsheaf *and* Plough *is our country's delight,*
For the Rose and Crown *St.* George *will still fight.*
And the Bull's Head *will soon the Frenchman dismay,*
At the bark of the Dog *they will all run away.*
We will beat him by land and still will be free,
And with our fair Ships *we will beat him by sea.*
We will beat all the Frenchmen and Russians to Boot,
And drown all invaders we can't manage to shoot.

Let us still with true courage unite and be free,
For we will be masters both by land and by sea.
And we will each one and all with the <u>Nightingale</u> sing
Our Army, our Navy, our Country, our Queen.

[It's interesting to note that, of the 32 pubs named (there were two pubs called the Ship), only the Highlander, the Cock, the Sun, the Red Hart and the Rose and Crown are still trading under the names they held in 1867. Some have changed names – the Adam and Eve has had two different buildings on adjoining plots, and a total of four different names: the Tut and Shive, *the* Phoenix *and the* Venue *before its demolition in 2020. Others have also been demolished, whilst some are now private dwellings or retail premises. SLW]*

Volume 13 no 2, February 2003

Hitchin's First Train

By John Scorer

John Scorer (HSME member, formerly H&DMEC) researched the replica train from the 1951 Pageant. It was built by the Hitchin and District Model Engineering Club, *which became the* Hitchin Society of Model Engineers, *and then sadly folded. Ex-members Bob and Mick Frost were involved in the construction of the first train and were able to provide much invaluable information about it. The train featured in Episode 8 of the Pageant which was titled*

'The Age of Progress: the Railway Comes to Hitchin — 1850'

Hitchin Museum has a collection of photos of the train. These were donated by Mrs. Margaret Payne, of Stevenage, who was a step-daughter of Eric Peters, who was one of the members involved and who is seen in some of the photos. I got in touch with Mrs. Payne who gave a few details of her step-father, whom she recalled as having mentioned Club members Bob and Mick Frost, and Frank Grainger.

Research initially consisted of looking through the Museum's newspaper archive for the period. This produced much useful information, mainly obtained from the Pageant special edition of the *Herts & Beds Express.*

Fortunately, both Bob and Mick Frost are still alive and well and were able to provide details of the construction and operation of the train.

Whilst the basis of the research was initially to satisfy my own curiosity, it has been suggested that the results should be put into print, so that a record is available for others with an interest in local and railway history.

To complete the story, it is intended that the record includes relevant details of the Pageant, and the names and reminiscences of the actors/actresses who participated in the episode.

Above: H&DMEC members in front of the locomotive. (L to r):- Reg Morgan, Bob Frost, Eric Peters, Eric Keith, 'Jenks' Jenkins (Club secretary & Project team leader), George Vandyke, John Mitchell, Mr. Purchass, Frank Grainger (Club treasurer), Mick Frost. (John Scorer)

The first three of the photographs from the Museum's collection show participants in front of the train. Are you included, or do you know anyone who is? I will be interested to hear from you. Also of interest will be to which local organization each participant belonged. The organizations involved in Episode 8 were:- Hitchin Youth Centre, St.Ippolyts Women's Institute, St. Ippolyts Drama Group, R.A.F. Henlow; Sub-producer Tom Baldry; Jessie Crawley (secretary); Violet Mayhead (wardrobe).

Notes of the train construction and operation follow. These show that details of the construction of the coaches, including their colour scheme, are lacking. What is also unknown is how the train 'split' was arranged. The train coupling was made to fail as a start away from the station was made, as was noted in the Pageant programme:-

After a few preliminary grunts, the train starts off. The people cheer wildly. JOE WALTERS: Look! Half of the train has been left behind. You don't get that on a coach.

And it is true. Half the coach has been left behind. The train backs, the carriages are linked up, and the train starts off again.'

Above, right and the following page: three pictures of the train, with passengers in period costume. (John Scorer)

Above: another picture of the train, with passengers in period costume. (John Scorer)

Do you know anything about these aspects? Do you have any unpublished photos, especially colour ones? Any help will be much appreciated.

Train Construction & Operation

A group of members met on Saturday afternoons to build the train. Construction, which took some time, took place in a barn, believed to be called 'The Kennels'. This was located on the Priory Estate, about halfway up Hitchin Hill and approximately opposite the junction with Standhill Road. This location was important, as when the train moved from the barn to be ready for the Pageant, it only had to move a short distance without the need to travel on a public road.

It is believed that the design of the locomotive was based on photographic evidence. The locomotive was built around a Fordson tractor and a two-wheeled cart. The side frames of the locomotive were made from two large wooden beams which were attached either side of the tractor.

The rest of the engine was built up on this chassis, using hardboard, plywood and possibly cardboard. The chimney top was an old enamel washing up bowl.

It is recalled that John Mitchell took great care in painting the front buffer beam with `No.1' on it. The locomotive colour scheme was Brunswick green with yellow lining and red buffer beams.

Each of the two coaches was built on a farm trailer. No information about the construction or paint scheme of the coaches has so far been run to earth. Note from the photos that the coaches did not appear to have roofs.

The train made a single circuit of the road around the Park. The spectators were in the centre, and could only see one side of the train, this side only being fully finished. This enabled Pete Hudson, sitting on the 'blind' side of the train, to operate his model boiler, burning things like roofing felt to provide lots of steam and good black smoke.

We have already mentioned both the Club secretary, Mr. Jenkins who was Project team leader and the Club treasurer, Frank Grainger, as being involved in the project; other members who were involved were Bob and Mick Frost.

Reg Morgan had a car electrical business in Florence Street (his wife still owned the property in later years).

George Vandyke was a relative of Frank Grainger and lived in Lancaster Avenue.

Mr Purchass lived on Willian Road in the first property on the left after crossing the Letchworth boundary. He had a smallholding and grew blackcurrants.

John Mitchell held a staff position (as editor, possibly) on a model railway magazine, possibly the Model Railway Constructor.

Eric Peters lived in a Victorian house beside Kingshott School. Eric worked on a farm at Wymondley and later did grass cutting for the Council. Later he worked at County Workshops at Hatfield.

Pete Hudson (not shown in photograph) was for many years plant maintenance engineer with W. J.Rendell Ltd., of Ickleford Manor.

Volume 13 no 2, February 2003

School Reminiscences

By Mrs M D Newman

Memories are such fleeting things, and one of the things that the Hitchin Journal has done well over the years is preserve some of them that might otherwise have been lost. Mrs M D Newman, of Regal Court, Hitchin, provided some wonderful memories of a long-lost building in Hitchin and of a person who was very special to her:

We settled in Hitchin in 1914, when I was 2 years old, at 8, Baliol Road, opposite St.Michael's College. A bedroom overlooked the playing fields, which were the whole length of the road. We four children spent many hours watching the boys, and in the summer one boy in particular. He was a big lad, a wonderful athlete and an excellent high-jumper. He had a habit of pulling up his trunks before each run — hence our nickname for him — 'Pulley-up-trucks'. He was the Head Boy, George Beck. He left; a few years later he returned as a 'brother', and after many years he became Headmaster. He left the school eventually and stayed in the Ministry. We gained news of him every few years. He became a bishop, and finally our dear Pulley-up-trucks became the first Archbishop of the new Liverpool Cathedral. He died a few years ago.

We used to collect beech nuts from the beautiful beech trees at the bottom of the playing fields for our mother to make some kind of pudding in the First World War.

My eldest brother went to St Mary's Boys School before going on to the Boys' Grammar School — Jabez King was Head there at that time!

My two sisters went to St. Saviour's for a year before moving to 'Miss Sharp's' (Brand Street, Old Workmens' Hall, next door to Chalkley's). I was too young to remember much about that, but I remember going to meet them out of school - such a long walk! Later we used to chase two girls up Verulam Road till they turned in at the Convent, and we kept running till we reached the Girls' Grammar School! Memories? Oh yes!

One of the girls we chased also lives in Regal Court with me — alas girls no longer!

Volume 13 no 2, February 2003

The Maples Hospital

This article, taken from a Hitchin Girls' Grammar School magazine of 1916, gives a good illustration of activity in the town during the Great War. The Hospital occupied a house that once stood on the site of Waitrose/Maples Court at the corner of Old Park Road and Bedford Road.

The Maples Hospital is one of the Military Convalescent Hospitals attached to the First General Eastern Hospital at Cambridge and it was opened on April 15th, 1915.

The house, which is admirably suited for a small hospital, is let, at a reduced rent, to the 26th Herts Voluntary Aid Detachment by Mrs. William Hill. As long as five years ago a list was taken of furniture, bedding, etc., that would be lent to the Detachment to furnish a Voluntary Hospital in Hitchin in case of war. The furnishing of the entire Hospital is due to the fulfilment of these promises.

The Hospital contains six wards, accommodating twenty-four patients, and an orderly supplied by the St. John Ambulance Brigade, who sleeps in the house each night.

There are two large, airy day and dining rooms, and in one of these is a small billiard table given by the Hon. A. Holland Hibbert, County Director. This affords endless amusement to the patients from the time they are well enough to use it until the very hour - or, as is often the case, minute – they leave. Two cloak rooms, a boot room, two "wash-houses," and sanitary arrangements, of which even exacting War Office Officials approve complete the patients accommodation.

There is also a small surgery which approaches as nearly to the ideal as any place, not specially built for the purpose, can do. With its well-scrubbed shelves and floor, its spotless white paint, its commodious and well stocked cupboards and drawers, and its shining brass, nickel and glass fittings, it is indeed the pride of the Nurses' hearts. The part of the house occupied by the Staff is completely shut off from that used by patients. This comprises three bedrooms and three private rooms - two of which are used as offices and the third as a Staff sitting and dining room. In the basement is a large kitchen, scullery and larder, and beyond is ample cellar room.

The Hospital is staffed by the 26th Herts Voluntary Aid Detachment, assisted by the Weston Detachment.

Mrs. Clemens Usher, the Commandant, assisted by Miss Tiddeman, the Weston Commandant (in the absence of Miss Tindal Lucas) is responsible for the nursing arrangements.

Miss Phillips, the Quartermaster, and Miss Bristow, the assistant Quartermaster, have charge of everything to do with the housekeeping and commissariat. Nurses are on duty for a fortnight at a time and cooks for a week. An afternoon nurse comes each day and also a masseuse.

Two ladies as housemaids come each morning to clean that part of the house used by the Staff, while three daily act as kitchen maids working three hours each. Two ladies come on Monday afternoons and do the patients' mending.

The whole of this work is entirely voluntary and it is only to scrub floors that a charwoman is required.

During the time the Hospital has been open it has been inspected on various occasions by Surgeon-General Price, Surgeon-General Jenckins, Colonel Openshaw and other War Office Inspectors, and each has expressed himself well satisfied with everything.

The patients are sent to the Hospital from the Base Hospital at Cambridge and they are sent back there when their treatment is complete. Up to date one hundred and forty-four patients have been treated and of these about 85% have been cases of wounds — all requiring dressing.

Many of the patients are most interesting and all seem to enjoy the comparative freedom and good food. The way in which the food disappears is surprising and certainty most flattering to the cooks. Attached to the Hospital is a lovely garden, and there, during the summer months, the men thoroughly enjoyed playing clock-golf, bowls, skittles, and even cricket and football.

Mrs. Walter Carling has arranged three concerts weekly ever since the opening of the Hospital. These the men have much appreciated, for "Tommy" is nothing unless musical (or noisy).

Many friends, too, have invited the men to tea on one day a week – in many cases, taking them for delightful motor drives beforehand.

Others send vegetables, eggs, fruit, cakes, etc., and all this adds to the pleasant working of the Hospital.

That the men appreciate what is done, and that all the work involved is worthwhile, can be clearly seen in the many letters received from past patients. They not only write once, as a sort of duty, but many times, and they evidently look upon the Sisters and Staff as friends.

Several of the School Staff have helped at the Hospital and the following Old Girls:-

D. Bowman	M. Browne
Mrs. Crabbe (D. Spurr)	M. Flint
C. Gatward	M. Goldsmith
U. Hailey	V. Hailey
M. Hall	E. Hatch
K. Little	Mrs. Shillitoe (H. Sale)
D. Snell	W. Snell
B. Spurr	M. Warren
Mrs. Widdows (C. Bennett)	E. Witter
Q. Wright	Mabel Hall
S. Fife	Patty Hall
A. Lucas	J. Hall
R. White	

Volume 13 no 2, February 2003

Hitchin's Town Halls

As They Were... and as They Might Have Been!

Derek Wheeler

I promised you some time ago that I would show you some alternative designs for the New Town Hall. Whilst searching for one of the designs, by Geoffry Lucas, I found this lovely picture of the Bedford coach galloping down Brand Street.

Above: The Bedford coach and the old Town Hall.   Below: the Lucas design, which was drawn in 1898, shows how narrow Grammar School Walk was then, with high garden walls either side. (North Hertfordshire Museum)

Volume 13 no 3, October 2003

News From Down Under

Terry Knight

It can be said, in all honesty, that history is all around us, quite often under our feet. This has certainly been the case in Bucklersbury and Sun Street where, during the enhancement work being carried out in those two roads, a number of gulley gratings made by three former Hitchin ironmongers, John Gatward & Son, G. H. Innes, and Innes, Sons & King have been revealed.

John Gatward & Sons was a firm of engineers established in 1835. Its ironmongery store stood on the High Street side of the entrance to the Swan Inn yard and an iron foundry was run from behind what is now the Arcade. When the Swan closed in 1884 it was bought and modified by John Gatward and by adding a glazed roof he was able to use the enclosed area as a furniture storeroom. The firm continued in business until it was sold to make way for the shopping arcade, which opened in 1927.

G. H. Innes originated in the Market Place but moved to Walsworth Road at the beginning of the twentieth century. During the First World War an American, originally called Harry Mayer, who later wished to be known as George Walter King, took over the company, which subsequently became known as Innes, Sons & King.

Information for this article was obtained from *Discovering Hitchin*, edited by Priscilla Douglas and Pauline Humphries and published by Egon Publishers in 1995.[1]

Above left: a gully drain cover by Innes & King. Right, a gas cover by Gatward. (Scilla Douglas)

---

[1] A second volume, *Discovering More About Hitchin*, edited by Bridget Howlett and Pauline Humphries, was published by Hitchin Historical Society in 2018. See **www.hitchinhistoricals.org.uk** for details.

Volume 13 no 3, October 2003

Frost On My Window Pane… and
Downstairs As Well!

Derek Wheeler

In the Autumn of 1967, by way of a slump in family fortunes, three Wheelers, mother, father and your worthy Editor found themselves homeless, and by the rapid revolution of the wheel of fortune, soon found themselves living in a very comfortable, indeed, bespoke, abode.

The late Charlie Frost and his wife Hazel, kindly rented us the flat above the Frost's cycle shop in Walsworth Road. I must say that the year I spent there was one of the happiest in my life. Since I had a collection of Victorian bicycles to store and restore, the Frost backyard, where I was allowed to keep my workbench and tools was an ideal environment wherein to pursue a hobby, although Mrs Day who lived above the fruiterer's shop next door was heard to remark in her own inimitable fashion, after a particularly long period of enduring me using a five-pint brazing blowlamp,

"He's either making a noise or a smell, that boy".

The Frosts encouraged my eccentric behaviour and I got on particularly well with an elderly neighbour of theirs, from Trevor Road, called Fred Bullard. Whenever I got home from teaching at Queen Street School, Fred would be in the cycle workshop talking to Charlie about the state of Britain and whether or not Mrs such-and-such should really be allowed out on her own! He always left at the shop's closing time, leaving a trail of tobacco smoke behind him and loudly murmuring that he was going to have kippers and custard again for tea today! Fred's daughter is the talented local artist Leslie Dargert.

Graham Frost was at this time still at school but I have known him since he was five years old, being a friend of a young cousin of mine. Having known the family for so long, it is a privilege for me to include a potted history of the firm in this journal, since it has now reached its half-century.

Charles Frost set up in business, in Bridge Street in Hitchin, in 1953, when there were at least half a dozen cycle shops in the town. The shop moved to its present site at 94 Walsworth Road, in 1959. It expanded to take in the adjacent shop in 1971, and in 1989 enlarged its premises yet again to provide a new workshop, and a clothing department. Charlie's son Graham joined the family business in 1977, and after the death of his father in 1983, Graham took on Paul Bullen as his business partner.

The shop now employs three full-time, and one part-time, members of staff, both male and female.

Every aspect of cycling is now catered for. Both new and second-hand cycles are sold, and, in addition repairs are carried out, also servicing and refurbishment. The shop also sells all things that go with a bike, from puncture outfits to computers.

Cycles are only sold from manufacturers whose product is of proven quality, and who can give the firm back-up in the form of spares and technical advice. The companies currently dealt with are Brompton, Diamondback, Raleigh, Ridgeback and Specialized.

By using these very different manufacturers it is felt that the firm can cater for every cyclist, from one-year-old tricyclists, enthusiastic teenagers, mad-keen off-roaders, the shopping mother, to the ex-racing grandfather.

The most important aspect of the business is service. All work carried out on cycles, whether it is new cycle preparation, or a repair, is done by one mechanic, and checked by a second. They in no way want to sell a bike and then never see it or its owner again. In fact they encourage the opposite. For a start, before the cycle has ever been ridden it is completely checked over and lubricated in the Frost workshop. Then, for a small charge, the customer can take out their Service Scheme. This entitles him or her to bring the cycle back after two months and thereafter each year for a service, for as long as they own the bike.

Repairs and servicing can be done on any cycle. They maintain a vast stock of parts, wheels, tyres, tubes, chainwheels etc. For a small charge, repairs can be collected, and in the summer, as things hot up, they also operate a booking system, so that a bike has to be off the road for as little time as possible.

They don't just sell bikes, they have a full range of clothing, including helmets, tops, shorts, longs, gloves, socks, shoes, boots, and accessories such as computers, glasses etc...

Frosts hold an annual sale every January. This year being their Golden Jubilee will be something very special!

(With many thanks to Graham Frost for providing the above information).

[At the time Derek was writing, Frost's Cycles in Walsworth Road, close to the junction with Trevor Road, was a thriving concern. It has since been taken over by one of Frost's employees under the name of Paul's Bikes. SLW]

THE CYCLE DEPÔT.

JOHN T. CHALKLEY,

BRAND STREET, HITCHIN.

AGENT FOR

Humber, Singer, .

Sunbeam, Star,

&c., &c. . .

Cycles of every description.

REPAIRS by skilled workmen. MACHINES LET ON HIRE.

Old Machines taken in exchange.

Above: Chalkley's supplied bicycles in Brand Street for many years. This advertisement dates from 1899.

Volume 13 no 3, October 2003

The Hitchin Physic Garden

Deirdre Boggon, Designer and Curator of the Hitchin Physic Garden

If Vi Lewis had not had the foresight to put into store the fittings and contents of her chemist shop when it closed down in 1961, Hitchin would be without a unique display and garden at the Museum.

After a public fund raising exercise in the town in the 1980s, the Perks and Llewellyn chemist shop was reconstructed at the Museum, complete with its mahogany fittings, bottles, jars and ephemera as a unique and original representation of a Victorian chemist's.

To complement the shop, a garden of medicinal plants was created from a patch of lawn between the Museum and Paynes Park. This is no ordinary physic garden, for in its design and planting a whole history of Hitchin is displayed.

Above: The pestle and mortar sundial in the Physic Garden in late July 2020. There are plants that are poisonous, and others, like rue, which should not even be touched (rue can cause blistering). There is a warning notice on the gate. (SLW)

To demonstrate the uniqueness of this garden, let us look first at its design. The garden has a pleasing balance of York stone paths, borders, Victorian benches and a unique and unusual sundial forged in bronze from a large pestle and mortar. Framed by cast iron railings, a yew hedge gives the garden a feeling of enclosure and intimacy. These railings, together with the handsome cast iron gates were forged at Henry Isaac's in St Ippolyts. The well-proportioned York paving was rescued from the Priory when a car park was being constructed on the site of a derelict Gertrude Jekyll sunken garden. The two cast iron benches much used by visitors, especially at lunchtime, are based on a grape vine design and again were cast by Henry Isaac.

The borders are divided into categories-external ailments, internal ailments, household and culinary usage. In total there are 100 different species of plant in the garden. The local connection continues. Hitchin's once important lavender industry is represented by a swathe of Hidcote lavender edging the central path. The two central borders are dedicated to William Ransom and contain plants grown by this Hitchin chemist and farmer in the fields around the town to use in his chemist shop in the early 19th century-field poppies, marigolds, chamomile, aconite and Pasque flower. To add to his range of pharmaceutical preparations, William Ransom established contact with merchants who imported plants from all over the world in the form of roots, bark and stems, and some of these plants can also be seen in the William Ransom borders - coneflower (Echinacea), elecampe, bistort, podophyllum and cascara[1]. Ransom's today is a thriving modern company producing a wide range of drugs, medicines and galenicals for the food, cosmetic and pharmaceutical industries – all plant based.

It was important that the garden should be as colourful as possible and also easy to maintain. Some medicinal plants, although wild flowers in their natural habitat, are nothing but dull, nuisance weeds in a garden situation. With careful selection, and taking into consideration the light, free-draining soil that we have in Hitchin, a collection was devised that is colourful and well behaved. Some plants are familiar as garden plants – foxglove, paeony, pansy, strawberry, colomon's seal - but their medicinal use came much before their ornamental use in our gardens. There is not a month in the year when something is not in flower – even in mid-winter, but the garden comes into its true glory in the early summer when the rose hedges are in bloom. These were deliberately placed adjacent to the pavement leading to the Museum and Library. Two species were chosen: Rosa gallica – the Apothecary's rose, and Rosa damascena – the Damask rose, used in the making of Attar of Roses. Both have heady perfumes and when in full flower their scent wafts across the path to delight passers-by. Add to this spectacle the strong colours of the lavender, the field poppies, the dyer's greenweed, the marigolds and the foxgloves and few passers-by can resist turning their heads to look.

The Hertfordshire Medical and Pharmaceutical Museum Trust was formed in the late 1980s to ensure the future of the garden and the chemist shop. Thirteen years on the garden will undergo extra maintenance this winter in terms of replacing or dividing overgrown specimens and replenishing the soil. Normal maintenance is carried out by a team of dedicated volunteers who work for just one or two hours a week on a rota basis and it is thanks to them that the garden is cared for and thus appreciated by its visitors.

There are not many times in the day when someone isn't wandering around the garden or sitting on the bench enjoying this little colourful and scented oasis in town. Local school children visit to draw from the information provided about the plants and the part they have played in the medical and pharmaceutical history of this town. A Lavender Fair is held each

---

[1] The Cascara tree did not grow well. In 2015 it was replaced by a Hitchin Pippin apple tree.

year with the garden as a centrepiece. There is a Vi Lewis Memorial Lecture during the Hitchin Festival where a guest speaker is invited to talk on a subject relating to medicinal plants, and regional television companies make regular visits to film the garden for a topical feature.

In creating this unique garden not only is Hitchin's history of plant medicine preserved but also an amenity has been given to the town for all to enjoy.

Volume 13 no 3, October 2003

Memories of an Evacuee in Hitchin

Mrs Barbara Hall (nee Budd)

The very first thing that I remember clearly about this time of my life was meeting at our school, Hornsey Road School, London, and being marched 'crocodile style' to the railway station at Finsbury Park.

My mum and three sisters were going to be evacuated all together, but at the last minute these plans were changed as our Headmistress, Miss Phair, said that she was unable to come along as her mother was poorly. My mum volunteered to stay behind and look after her mother, as Mum considered it more important that our headmistress be with the children she taught. The only thing that Mum insisted upon was that my two older sisters and myself should be kept together when we arrived in Hitchin. That meant that my younger sister stopped in London with Mum.

When we finally arrived in Hitchin we all were sent to a large hall where the host families were waiting for us.

The first family we were sent to stay with was Mrs Terry, in Bearton Road, and I must say I was thoroughly spoilt, as I was a sickly child. But all good things came to an end and we were then sent to another family, who only wanted us for the money, and so we only stayed there for two weeks!

After this we were placed with Mr and Mrs Sell at Kershaws Hill. We stayed with these people until they moved away to Ware.

On again, to another family – Mrs Patmore at South Place, Red Hill Road. We were happy there. I remember that one of my sisters had to have her tonsils out, and was sent to what we called the camp hospital. We were allowed to wave to her through the wire fence. I remember that the men in the camp wore blue uniforms.

During this time away, I became ill with rheumatic fever and chorea (St. Vitus's Dance) and I was taken into a large house that had been converted into a hospital for the evacuees. I was once again spoilt rotten by the staff. If I wanted the cuffs from Matron's uniform I was given them! Whatever I wanted I received.

We were not allowed to go into the General hospital, but I was very happy in the big house. We could play in the garden and we were allowed to make mud pies too. During the time I was there my sisters returned to London.

Another thing I clearly remember about my stay in Hitchin is going to church three times on a Sunday, and that was something new, as we didn't do that in London.

I spent most of my childhood in children's hospitals, but I will never forget my stay in Hitchin. Although I was only 6 years old when I was evacuated, I believe that experience in the country never really left me.

My husband and I have now settled in Kelvedon in Essex.

Was the "camp hospital" the old Lister, which had a wire fence round its barracks, or was it the hospital at Henlow Camp? Was the big house "The Maples" in Bedford Road, which was next door to the "General," as Mrs Hall calls the old North Herts Hospital? It certainly had a very large garden. I went there as an infant to attend eye clinics. (Derek Wheeler).

Volume 14 no 1, February 2004

The Regal Cinema: Demolition

Above: the Regal in 1985, taken from Skynner's Almshouses, not long before demolition. (Andrew Wearmouth)

Above: A scene viewed from the balcony of the 'Regal' Cinema which no cinema goer ever saw – the end of an era for Hitchin. (Colin Dunham)

Volume 14 No. 1, February 2004

Who Was Who in 1916

I came across a little book which was entitled 'Pictorial Record-Hitchin, Letchworth and Stevenage'. I think it dates from the middle of World War 1. I have included an extract which lists some of the traders and dignitaries who were prominent during that time. The readers may find the following interesting. When one is writing a history of those times it is useful to use such articles for the purpose of cross-referencing against known details. (Derek Wheeler)

W. & S. LUCAS, Ltd., Brewers and Bottlers, Mineral Water Manufacturers, and Wine and Spirit Merchants, The Brewery, Sun Street, Hitchin - Tracing the origin of the Hitchin Brewery of Messrs. W. & S. Lucas, Ltd., we are carried as far back as the year 1709, when it was established by Isaac Grey, whose daughter was married to the first William Lucas to be connected with the firm. As the years have rolled on this brewery has moved with the times in every way; has extended the premises, improved and increased the plant, added a mineral water manufactory, cultivated a spirit trade, acquired licensed houses-which now represent about two –thirds of its trade-and in 1898 became a limited liability company. The Chairman of the directors is Mr. Samuel Lucas, and the other directors, Mr. William Lucas (his second cousin) and Mr. Samuel Lucas, jun. Mr Samuel Lucas is Chairman of the Barnsley Brewery Co. also. He lives at 'Tilehouse,' an ancient picturesque residence in Tilehouse Street, a few minutes' walk from the brewery, and takes an active interest in all that goes on there and in the town, to the public well-being of which he has contributed by service on the Council for a period of six years or so, and for twenty-two years as hon. secretary of the North Herts and South Beds Hospital. The manager of the brewery is Mr. George Taylor, who has been in its service for thirty-two years.

C. W. THAKE, Newsagent and Stationer, 16, Sun Street, Hitchin - The small, double-fronted shop in Sun Street where Mr. Charles William Thake started business in 1899, is one, of those places whither people are accustomed to repair who appreciate a pleasant word, along with, of course, the right article at the right price. Mr. Thake is not only the personification of the genial manner, but he thoroughly knows his trade, as indeed, he should do, for he was apprenticed to it here in his native town with the late Mr. Charles Hales as far back as the year 1875. Mr. Thake has a large delivery connection of newspapers and a well-stocked shop of papers, stationery, picture post cards, etc., Miss Thake assisting in the business.

W. WHALEY & SON,
Hairdressers and Ornamental Hair Manufacturers, The Q.C.C. Central Toilet Saloon, Market place, Hitchin - It is forty-two years since Mr. William Whaley, who is a native of St. Ives, succeeded North at the Sun Street corner of the Market Place, and North was here for a long period. When in earlier years engaged with Banes, at Southampton,

MR. WILLIAM WHALEY.

MR. WILLIAM F. WHALEY.

THE LATE MR. FK. JOHN WHALEY.

MR. P. H. WHALEY.

Mr. Whaley had the honour of cutting the hair of General Gordon and many other celebrities. He has known two generations of customers in Hitchin and has been active in connection with the movement for early closing, with the Choral Society, etc. His eldest son, Mr. Wm. F. Whaley, who has had experience at Worthing and other fashionable resorts, and at High Wycombe, and who has been a special constable from the time of the origination of that force, is now a partner. Mr. Whaley's second son, Mr. Fredk John Whaley, has given his life for his country in the course of the " Great Push " in August, 1916. He was a private in the Wessex

R.F.A. Mr. Percy Hugh Whaley, Mr. Whaley's youngest son, is a private in the Herts R.F.A., and is now in India. Ornamental hair manufacturing is carried on the premises, and upstairs is a ladies' hairdressing saloon, fitted with electric driers, appliances for Marcel waving, etc. Hot and cold baths may be had at any time, and a large business is done in this line-and in fancy goods dealing, umbrella re-covering, etc. The Q.C.C. in the designation of the business stands for Quick, Clean, and Comfortable.

HOBLEY'S, Bakers, Confectioners and Caterers, Market Square, Hitchin - In addition to its being a place for the consumption of delicacies, for teas and for banquets, Hobley's affords to the tourist one of the sights of Hitchin. A house, built in Tudor days, with old beams bearing Tudor dates, could certainly claim to be worth seeing even if the viands were not worth consuming. This, however, is, a first class confectioner's shop, where everything is of the best, where coffee grinding and roasting has been made a feature, and it is a celebrated catering establishment. There is upstairs an ancient banqueting hall, about 18 yards long by 6 yards wide, a hall capable of seating nearly 700 persons; with old oak beams. It is a room that otherwise impresses the memory-by reason of the hideous face that adorns one of the walls.

There is a smoking-room on the same floor and a coffee-room, where what is known as a powder cupboard was discovered in one corner. Hobley's has not always been Hobley's; for many years it was Logsdon's, and, indeed, it is now Hobley's in name only. The proprietor is Mr. S.E. Hayter, who also owns the old-established catering business of " Hobley's," at 18, High Street, Rugby. Tele. No. 118

JOHN McINTOSH, Motor Engineer, Exchange Yard, Hitchin - Mr. John McIntosh was apprenticed to the engineering trade in his native town of Coupar Angus, Scotland, and in various examinations in engineering at Dundee and Forfar evening classes secured all grades of certificates in engineering. He commenced business a few years ago in Hitchin, and has a well fitted workshop with lathes, etc., driven by a 2 h.-p. gas engine.
Those -whose motor cars stand in need of repairs of any kind may at Exchange Yard obtain the services of a thoroughly practical man, of whose competence there is no question.

T. L. RABAN, Saddler and Harness Maker, 17, High Street, Hitchin - Mr. Raban can with legitimate pride show a piece of leather bearing the date 1740, and an old box with the mark 1798 thereon, both mementoes of the early days of the business carried on by him for the last twenty years in the present premises, and for twenty years before at premises not far away in the same street. He was apprenticed with his uncle, W. C. Raban, and succeeded to the latter's business. Paddon was an earlier principal here, and before him was Topham. The shop faces directly down Brand Street, and at the rear is a roomy workshop. Mr. Raban is a native of Olney. For thirty-seven years-up to three years ago-he was a member of the choir of Hitchin Church.

Right: Mr T L RABAN, saddler and harness maker, who operated from his premises on the High Street, Hitchin. Below, Herbert Moore was a tailor and outfitter for both gentlemen and ladies. His shop was also in the High Street.

HERBERT MOORE, High Class Outfitter and Ladies' and Gentlemen's Tailor, 11, High Street, Hitchin

Mr. Herbert Moore, who is a native of Wilton, in the county of Norfolk, has, since 1905, enjoyed an enviable position as the successor of Mr. Lawson Thompson in one of the oldest established businesses in the neighbourhood, commenced by Mr. Thompson's family well over a century ago. Mr. Moore gained his experience in Kensington, London, and in the provinces. . Since taking over this business he has largely remodelled and refitted the interior of the premises, also, moving with the times, he has added a ladies' tailoring department, which has proved a success. The workshops are on the premises, and the entire business is under the constant supervision of the principal. The cutting department maintains the high reputation that has always been enjoyed by this firm. The hosiery side is complete and modern in every respect. A speciality is made in ladies' and gentlemen's rainproofed coats, and a sole agency is held for the "Aquatite" proofed clothes. Mr. Moore has served as a special constable since the commencement of the war, and five of his staff have joined the Army.   (Moore's telephone number was Hitchin no. 2).

Above: Brand Street, Hitchin, by T B Latchmore

A. LANE & CO., High Class Cabinet Makers and Art Furnishers, Brand Street, Hitchin. For the past twelve or thirteen years there has been established opposite the 'Post Office a premier furnishing place, the tastefully arranged windows of which always attract the eye. Mr. Arthur Lane, the principal, has, in the period named, built up an extensive connection in Hitchin, and other parts of Hertfordshire. He supplies goods of the most reliable, as well as the most artistic, kind, and is himself an expert cabinet-maker, with the advantages attaching: to

experience in high class work in the West End. At the workshops: to the rear nothing inferior is ever produced, and none save furniture for the élite is allowed a place in the shop or the showroom on the first floor. Antique furniture is included in the stock, and besides cabinets proper, chairs, settees, etc., there are carpets, blinds, loose covers, and soft furnishings generally. A large selection of *repousse* work is always on hand, and an agency is held for Ickleford industries. Experienced men are sent out to fit linos that have been bought here. Mr. Lane is at any time glad to advise prospective customers as to the best methods of decoratively furnishing a house in accordance with its style and antiquity, and in further accordance with the outlay that the customer is prepared to spend on necessary articles, and on cosy corners and similar luxurious details.

NORTH HERTS AND SOUTH BEDS HOSPITAL, Bedford Road, Hitchin-The North Herts and South Beds Hospital has been housed on its present site since the year 1840. It took the place of an earlier dispensary for out-patients, which had been founded seventeen years previously. The building stands in its own grounds one minute's walk from Brand Street. A subscription of one guinea per annum makes the giver a governor, with option of exchanging one in-patient recommendation for four out-patients, or *vice versa*. Donations of £25 and upwards makes the donor a governor for life, while contributions of higher and lower degree are also welcomed. Gifts in kind may be made to the matron, Miss Hall. The Hon. Secretary is Mr. Lawson Thompson, a gentleman well known in the charitable, the civic, and the intellectual life of Hitchin. The Treasurer is Mr. Wm. Tindall Lucas; B.A.Oxon., J.P., of Barclay's Bank.

Volume 14 nos 1 & 2, February & October 2004

Not Just a Dry Old List of Names
A Look at the Registers of Hitchin British Boys' School, part I
1827-1877
Lyn Lloyd-Smith

I would like to share with you something of what I have learned from the indexing project that we have been working on here for the last two years. I am very much aware that many of you will know infinitely more about the history of Hitchin and indeed of the British Schools than I do but I hope that we will learn from each other, that I will enlighten you in some way and that you may be able to answer some of the questions I have.

First let me declare my interest. I approached Fiona Dodwell with a view to indexing the records because of my fascination with genealogy. Most people trace only their own family history but I have come to the conclusion that I am chronically nosy and want to find out about everyone else's as well! Creating an index makes a record more accessible and having made use of other people's indexes to track down some of my own ancestors, I saw this partly as a way of reciprocating.

Now many people are keen to acquire famous or wealthy ancestors. In some ways this is quite sensible, as someone who was well known will have much written about them that is easy to access. Take one Mr Frederick Ray Howkins of St Clair shores, Michigan, U.S.A. who through discovering that he was descended illegitimately from Charles the 2nd Duke of Lennox and Richmond can trace his male ancestry back to Alan, Hereditary Steward of Dol in Brittany in the 11th century and in the female line can go all the way back to the Shah of Persia in 191 AD. As you can imagine, he will probably be able to spend the rest of his life reading about his ancestors.

However there is also the apocryphal story told by a well-known genealogist of one of the students in his evening class, who was attracted to family history because of her family's belief that they were descended from the Duke of Buckingham. She had amassed a great deal of information on the descendants of this family over many years, only to find when she set about the research methodically that her great grandfather had kept a public house called the *Duke of Buckingham*! The innkeeper of the *Duke of Buckingham* may not have fought famous battles but his life will have been full of struggles that were equally interesting but have not necessarily found their way into the written word. For me this is the challenge and the fascination of records such as those of the British Schools; we touch the lives of the ordinary person, a brief entry in a school register can lead to a whole new area of research.

Jill Grey and the British Schools.

As many of you know the British Schools were founded in 1810 by William Wilshere to educate the children of the labouring poor of Hitchin, but the earliest register that survives is from 1827 for the Boys' School, the earliest Girls' School register is much later, from 1874. We owe the survival of these records to Jill Grey who devoted so much of her life to the preservation of the school. While the registers were in her possession she carried out much detailed analysis of their content.

In September 2001, I started indexing the 1827-1843 register and was soon joined by Sue Parsons, which helped to speed up the project considerably. We were able to check each other's work and obtain a higher degree of accuracy in so doing. At points we felt like intrepid explorers, an international team following in the footsteps of Jill Grey. We got to know a variety of locations in the British Schools; we endured extremes of temperature but were always looked after by Fiona, ever mindful of our comfort. We encountered difficulties along the way, principally in the form of handwriting…and that was just mine!

Writing, ah, writing and indeed spelling! What variety is encountered, but that is quite another story!

Transcription of Registers

What we have done, I referred to as indexing but in fact, we have transcribed the registers. This has served several purposes.

Firstly, it means that the original registers, which are in quite a fragile condition, do not need to be handled, as the information is available in transcript.

Secondly, being stored electronically and copied several times, the information they contain will be available forever.

Thirdly, it is possible to analyse the data quickly and easily. You can answer questions on the content of the registers simply by calling it up on the computer.

The information given as standard in the registers was as follows: -

> Surname of the child
> Christian name of the child
> Age of the child
> Religious denomination
> Father's occupation
> Address

Throughout the period covered there are various different ways of noting either the class the child is in, or the educational level he has obtained and I have not yet attempted to make sense of these.

Later from the 1860s, the father's Christian name is also given and the previous school which the child attended.

One point on which I can find no concrete evidence is who was the informant for the entries on the register. In many cases it was probably a parent but in some instances it may well have been the child himself. One entry where I felt the child himself must have been the informant was where the father was identified as an *'odd man'*. I have however since learnt that that really was an alternative form of *'odd job man'*.

The *Manual of the British and Foreign Schools Society* of 1833 gives guidance on what books should be kept by each school and interestingly requires that a register be kept of attendance at church. Here I quote

"It is essential to any child's continuance in the school that his parents or guardians see that he attends regularly every Sabbath-day a place of worship or Sabbath school. To record their attendance is the object of this report. The parent of each defaulter is seen and admonished; if the admission be often repeated, the child is excluded."

I have not come across any evidence of this system having been enforced in Hitchin but if someone knows differently, I would be interested to hear.

There are three registers involved, 1827-1843, 1843-1859 and 1859 to 1877. Each register contains roughly 1300 names. For ease of reference, I will refer to each one by its starting date.

Now the British Schools were not the only educational establishment in the town, so I was interested to set it in context. I knew that the attendance at the school in 1854 was 154 pupils; I therefore decided to take a look at the 1851 census. I whiled away a happy couple of hours at the library doing a count of the number of boys aged 7-13. This is not a scientific study but my estimate is that there were 522 boys in this age group in Hitchin making the number who attended the British School roughly 30% of the total.

So let us look at the information contained in the register.

Surname

Firstly surname. This is, of course the basic tool of the genealogist's trade, the clues that lead us to our past. What is most striking about the names at the British Schools is that none is particularly outstanding. In 1827-1843, 11 names have between 1 and 2% representation; most of these are the common names like Brown, Smith and Taylor but we also have the more local names such as Jeeves, Odell and Warboys.

In 1843-59 the most common names are Carter and Day, both representing 2% of the children. By 1859-1877, the Carters have disappeared but the Days are still there at 2%. Jeeves and Warboys have also disappeared but Odells are still there, albeit transformed to Irishmen! (*O'Dell*).

Here I must say thank you to Val Holland and Fiona who helped count the names. This is another area where much more analysis must be done.

A Look at the Registers of Hitchin British Boys' School part II
Lyn Lloyd-Smith

Next, Christian names. Now here I did learn something interesting. What do you think was the most popular boy's name in 19th century Hitchin? Well, the answer is that the leader, by a long shot and first choice for 20% of parents who sent their children to the British Schools between 1827 and 1843 was William, next was George with 13%, then John on 11.5%, then Charles, James and Thomas on around 8% each and Henry with 5%. Those seven names accounted for an amazing 75% of the children.

Over the period of the registers there is gradually more variety in the names given; so in 1843 – 1859 these names account for 65.5% of the children and in 1859 –1877 for 54%.

George gained more popularity mid-century but was overtaken again by William in the third register.

Apart from the more common Christian names, I have divided the names, which occur only once or twice in each register, into three categories i.e. Biblical names, historical names and surnames.

Firstly Biblical names, these include names that we think of as being very common today, such as Matthew, Mark, Stephen, Timothy and Peter, but also Ebenezer, Jabez, Levi, Absalom and Nimrod. 4% of the children in the 1827 – 43 register come into this category; this had risen to 7% by mid-century but fallen back to 3.7% by 1859 – 77. Was this perhaps to do with spiritual revival mid-century, which increased the interest in Biblical names? Perhaps someone has a theory on this?

The term 'historical' I use loosely to cover names from English history as well as Classical times. Given that most of his classmates were called Billy or Johnny or Jimmy, what must have been the feelings of the child who rejoiced in the name of Aquila? In the 1827 register only 18 children or 1.4% of the children had been so blessed by their parents, in the 1843 register 2.7% but by 1859 in line with the general trend for more variety this had risen to 3.3%.

In fact, the name Arthur which I include in the historical category in 1827 as it has only one representative, increases tremendously in popularity throughout the century. There are 14 in the 1843 register and 69 in the 1859 register. Francis and Frederick also come into this category.

By the 1859 register we are beginning to see names like Bernard and Norman, Sidney and Walter. I have to admit, at the risk of offending some of my audience, to thinking of these as old people's names but they were obviously new and trendy in the 1860s. It is, of course, very difficult to generalise from a small study like this but I would just like to make a comparison to research I have done in Ireland; while the names John and William and James are extremely common there also, at this period, frequently used names are Alexander, Hugh, Samuel, David, Andrew and Francis, many of which are hardly found at all in the British Schools Registers.

Religious Denomination

The only thing we can tell for sure in this category is the percentage of Church of England children who attended the school as a variety of names are used for the other denominations and we cannot now be sure exactly which Meeting was referred to – it may have been a Baptist or a Methodist. 62% of the 1827 children are Established Church, 49% of 1843 children and 41% of 1859 children. These numbers were of course affected by the opening of St Mary's National School in 1855 and St Saviours in 1868.

Should we feel sorry for the solitary Roman Catholic child registered at the school?

Father's Occupation

Now this is a fascinating area of study. As we have said, the school was founded for the children of the labouring poor and in the first register 40% of the fathers are said to be labourers, 17.5% in 1843. The 1859 register is more difficult to analyse in this way as much more information is given in this column, the father's Christian name and the name of his employer being often included, but it would be safe to say that many fewer gave their occupation as labourer.

However in reality there was always a wide range of occupations represented at the school. In the later period some are even what we would consider to be middle class. We have of course the butcher, the baker and if not a candlestick maker, we do have a chandler and many of the other common callings are there.

However, it is some of the more unusual ones, which draw the eye. What, for instance, is a higgler? In fact he was a pedlar, often with a horse and cart. One of the earliest occupations listed is in 1827, the father of William and Thomas Mansell who is a Man Midwife. We have other vaguely medical callings, for example in 1849 Richard Shillitoe's Dad is a Surgeon while in 1865 we have Mr.Culpin who combines the skills of Itinerant Minister and Homeopath. In the same year we have a Herbalist.

From medicinal to musical: in 1829 Mr. Maher is an organ builder, in 1856 Mr Anson is a Piano Forte tuner and showing us that the struggling musician is nothing new, in 1864 we have a Mr. Chote who is a bricklayer and musician.

The school also appeared to attract the children of the Nonconformist clergy. So as well as our itinerant Minister, there are also in the 1850s the children of the Wesleyan and Baptist Preachers and the Town Missionary.

Some interesting questions arise. For instance, was there a proliferation of wildlife in Hitchin in the late 1840s? We discover in the registers at this time three fathers who were a Mole Catcher, a Badger Killer and a Rat Catcher respectively.

The changing society of the 19th century is reflected in the occupations that come with technological progress. Gas was introduced in the town in 1834 but we do not have a gasfitter until 1856. Conversely, according to Reginald Hine, telegraph wires were fitted to the Post Office in 1869 yet we have an Electric Telegraph fitter, one Mr. Webb, in 1858; where did he work?

The coming of the railway in 1850 was of course an important event in the life of the town. Our first engine driver appears in 1851, the father of Rowland and Lewis Minns, and from then onwards there is a proliferation of Railway employees. In 1860, Frank Gale's father is a Railway Navigator, (i.e. a navvy) in Egypt and in 1863 George and Nicholas Swanson have waved goodbye to their father as he went to work as a Railway Engineer in Spain. Those family historians amongst you will have spotted that these last two are genealogical gems, which may help to explain the absence of an elusive ancestor.

There is a huge amount of information here which it would be impossible to cover in a talk like this so I will just close this category with the random fact that the first child of a photographer was Robert Berryman in 1861, twenty years after Fox Talbot patented his invention.

Address

Our final category is address. Here I must say a wholehearted thank you to Scilla Douglas. As someone who has lived in the area quite a short time, I needed much help on this one, and Scilla very kindly provided that and pointed me in the right direction.

I am grateful also to Brian Limbrick, who supplied me with a map of the town dated 1844. I have plotted as far as possible the addresses of the boys in the first two registers. By the third register it becomes much more difficult, partly because the town has grown considerably, but also because the variety of addresses makes this a project in itself.

Some obvious conclusions arise immediately on looking at the map. The majority of the pupils come from the surrounding area, Dead Street, Back Street, Tilehouse Street, and Bridge Street. There were many fewer children living in the Yards than I expected.

More children came from the outlying villages in 1827 than in 1843. This is no doubt that, as the century progressed, these villages had their own schools. Pirton, for example, had a British School from 1828 – 1833, and from 1842 a National School.

Now some addresses. Perhaps you can help me with these; Alpha Cottages, Bonfield Cottages, Boot Yard, Crabbs Close, Cross Keys, Gallaher's Yard, Harkins Hall, Higlors Hill, Steringay Road, Solomon's Temple, Soot Field Green, Thistley Farm, Joiners Folly, Rookery and Pondavix. I have to say that, as a result of doing this, my knowledge of the geography of Hitchin has increased tremendously. As I go round the town I think, 'Ah, so that is where......is'. [Ed: Alpha Cottages were opposite the Museum in Paynes Park, Boot Yard was in Bridge Street, Crabbs Close was opposite West Hill, now Waitrose car park. The Cross Keys was in Park Street, Soot Field Green is on the Charlton side of Preston. Perhaps our readers can help us out with the others?][1]

I hope this short talk has helped you to glimpse something of the community that existed at the British Schools in the 19th century.

Looking at a name on a piece of paper is one dimensional, we can know nothing of the delights or difficulties of the life that person led. By placing the name in context, however, we can begin to appreciate the richness and variety that existed.

The people of the 19th century may have been poorer than us, but they were no less inventive, argumentative, funny, idiosyncratic, grumpy and resourceful than our society in the 21st century. They were our ancestors and part of them has made us the people we are today.

Volume 14 no 2, October 2004

[I remember writing the following article. I had been researching what had really happened during the witchcraft trials of the 16 – 18th centuries for some time. It all started with a Peter Cook/Dudley Moore sketch in which it was alleged that suspected witches were "swum;" if they floated they were guilty, and they were hauled out, dried off and burned. If they sank and drowned they were innocent. This seemed to me that this seemed both unfair and unlikely, though it is still popularly believed. When I looked into it I found that it was indeed untrue. The research resulted in a book however – The Witches of Herfordshire, Tempus Publishing Ltd, 2004, ISBN 0 7524 3203 6. It was shortlisted for the Katherine Briggs Folklore Award of 2004, though the competition proved particularly strong that year, and it didn't win. SLW]

---

[1] "Gallaher's Yard was probably Hall's Yard in Tilehouse Street. Solomon's Temple was two cottages at the junction of Bancroft and Ickleford Road, later site of Frythe Cottages. Thistly Farm, Joiner's Folly, Pondywick Cottages and Harkers, or Harkness, Hall were in the parish of Ippollitts. (Bridget Howlett)

Elizabeth Lane: the White Witch of Walsworth
Simon Walker

Between the years 1542 and 1736 (with a short break during the reign of Edward VI), the practice of witchcraft was a crime in England. Before then, such matters were dealt with by the Ecclesiastical Courts; now, they were tried at Assize. Serious offences attracted the death penalty, by hanging.

Most people accepted the reality of the devil, evil spirits and witches. Should someone be taken unexpectedly ill, or some disaster occur on the farm, it was quite likely to be attributed to witchcraft. When that happened, there were a number of well-known precautions that could be taken – a horseshoe over the door, or a sprig of rowan wood for example – but the best cure was to consult a white witch.

These individuals went by a number of names; blessing witches, white witches, or cunning men or women. It was upon their skill and knowledge that ordinary folk relied, not just to save them from bewitchment, but for aid in a whole range of disasters. They could cure disease; find lost or stolen goods, and identify the thief; they could provide love potions; give an indication of future events, and so on. They were therefore much valued within most of the community.

There were some, however, that viewed them differently. Some thought them frauds: in 1627 Richard Bernard wrote that

> These VVitches, to keepe their credit, often deliuer their medicines with an If: If it doe no good, come againe. When they returne and finde that the Deuill hath not remoued the disease, or that God being displeased, will not let them; then the VVizards blame them, that they came not in time, or they applied not the meanes aright, or that they wanted faith to beleeue, or at least they acknowledged their power not great inough, and therefore they aduise them to goe to a more cunning

man or woman, and so direct them vnto another VVitch, or Deuill, for helpe, worse then themselues.[1]

Others objected for a different reason. In 1608, William Perkins expressed the view that they were worse than the black witches. The latter harmed only their victim's goods or corporeal body, whilst the white witch, whilst seeming good, was in fact in league with the devil, imperilling the eternal soul of their customers in an insidious manner. "Death therefore," he wrote, "is the just and deserved portion of the good Witch."[2]

But say what they might, cunning folk were generally popular, and rarely prosecuted. When they were, the reason was often their failure to perform. More unusual was Elizabeth Lane; she came to the attention of the courts as a result of what seems to have been a vendetta against a clergyman, John Knightly, of Guilden Morden. Whatever her reasons were, in the late 1590's she embarked upon a campaign of slander against Knightly. He in turn got to hear of her remarks, and gathered evidence against her, to present at the Quarter Sessions.

On 30 January 1598 he gave a recognizance before Thomas Docwra J P to appear and give evidence against Elizabeth, charging her with witchcraft. On the same day she gave a recognizance of £20 for her appearance; Richard Spede and Michael Wylkenson, or Wilkenson, both of Walsworth, gave recognizances of £10 each on her behalf, all substantial sums of money at the time. The evidence against her was substantial:

- John Smythe went to see her, because his wife was "in desperation," and was told by her that she was bewitched by "deep and profane learning" by Knightly.
- Robert Frost, troubled with a pain in his throat, visited her and was told that he was possessed by spirits and bewitched by John Knightley, but that she could help him; she received 16d and said he had promised to give her 6s 7d more.
- Joan Shatbolte admitted to the churchwardens that she had been to see Lane about her husband who was then ill, and was told that he was "beworded and bewatled" by Mr. Knightly, and she should cut off his hair and send her son with it to Lane. She should also turn his bed another way and throw his water on the fire. Shadbolt gave Lane 2s and a cheese. Her husband had since died.
- Thomas Payne went to her on behalf of his wife and paid her money, but was not prepared to say what actually happened.
- Walter Copis went to see her for a pain and said that she spoke evil words of the minister.
- Henry Wood went to see her about his horse that was stolen, for which she received money.
- John Kidd was sent to her by Anne, wife of Richard Lilley, with their daughter Grace.
- Elizabeth Follye, servant to Richard Lilley was sent by her mistress to see her with Grace Lilley, but she would not repeat what Elizabeth Lane said.

[1] Richard Bernard, A Guide to Grand Jurymen, (1627), Book II, chapter 9. Pp. 146/7
[2] William Perkins, A DISCOURSE OF THE DAMNED ART OF WITCHCRAFT... Printed by CANTRELL LEGGE, Printer to the Universitie of Cambridge. 1618. P.54

- Anne, wife of Richard Lilley, went to speak to her about her daughter, but she too refused to go into any detail of the meeting. Elizabeth Lane also went to her house to see her about things stolen from her buttery.
- Agnes Cooper went to her about a gown that had been stolen.
- Robert Shatbolt the elder went to see her because his wife was ill, and was told she was bewitched.

Kidd, Follye and Anne Lilley's visits are probably concerned with a childhood ailment in Grace Lilley.

The last reference we have of this affair is a clerk's note that Elizabeth Lane was to appear at the next Assizes. Wilkenson and Spede gave recognizances of £40 each that she would appear at the Assizes to answer the charges against her. Unfortunately there is no mention of her appearance at the Assizes, though the records for that year and the subsequent few years still exist. It may well be that the Grand Jury threw the case out, and any indictments were therefore discarded. As Lane and her supporters provided recognizances for her appearance, there would be no record of her in Gaol Calendars.

But that is not the last we hear of Elizabeth Lane. Some years later, in 1613, an "Elizabeth Laine" of Walsworth in Hitchin, described as a widow, and William Burr, husbandman, of Aspenden, entered recognizances to give evidence against Thomas and Agnes Hamond on a charge of witchcraft (they were acquitted). The hamlet of Walsworth was a pretty small place, not even meriting a church until the 1890s, so it seems likely that the two Elizabeths are one and the same person; this time though, she seems to be appearing on behalf of a prosecution, perhaps as an expert witness.

Other Sources:

1. Cecil l'Estrange Ewen, *Witch Hunting and Witch Trials*, Kegan, Paul, Trench, Trubner & Co. Ltd., 1929. The Hamonds were accused of, on 10 October 1608, bewitching 3 horses "of the goods and chattels of Edward Parker." The Grand Jury returned a true bill, but the Hamonds were acquitted. Ewen estimated that about 77% of records for the whole of the Home Circuit survive.
2. Hertfordshire Archives and Local Studies: They appear under the reference HAT/SR. Helen Browne appears in HAT/SR 1, and Elizabeth Lane under HAT/SR 10.

Volume 14 no 2, October 2004

Hermitage Road, Late Nineteenth Century

The photograph on the following page was taken in the late nineteenth century. The building left of centre is, of course, the Hermitage, home of Mr Frederic Seebohm and his family. It was Seebohm who donated the land for Hermitage Road to the town, reportedly to provide a shorter route to the railway station. Seebohm owned land on both sides of the road, and in 1874, George Beaver, the surveyor, reported that plans had been drawn up for Hitchin Local Board to build a tunnel to carry the river Hiz beneath the new road. This tunnel still exists, and is far larger than the more modern entrances at each end might suggest. There is room for not only the river but a footpath beside it as well.

The state of the road in Bancroft clearly leaves something to be desired; this part of the road was used for a route to the cattle market at the time, so it may be that the surface is more than just mud…

Right: The junction of Bancroft and the newly built Hermitage Road to the right. The building is the Hermitage, the home of Frederick Seebohm. (North Herts Museum Service)
Below: the tunnel carrying the Hiz beneath Hermitage Road, designed by George Beaver in 1874. This view is looking from the north, and the footpath once used by Seebohm is visible on the right. (SLW)

Brickyards in Hitchin, 1891

The *Journal of the Hitchin Natural History Club* for December 1891 carried an article by William Hill, FGS, entitled "Our Forgotten Lake." Hill argued that the presence of particular geological deposits to the south of the town were evidence of a long extinct lake. The evidence for these deposits came from excavations at various brick yards. The following is an extract:

In the south-east corner of the parish of Hitchin, in that part known as the Folly, are several brick yards. These are situated on the southerly slope of an irregular ridge or spur running about north-east and south-west, which form the eastern boundary of the valley in which Hitchin stands, and also the water-shed between the river Hiz and the little rivulet known as Ippolyts brook. This brook joining forces with the Pur at Purwell Mill, passes round the extremity of the spur, and becomes confluent with the Hiz at Grove Mill.

From the higher portions of the spur, that is across the park, along the cemetery ridge towards Highbury and the station, the ground sinks rapidly towards the valley of the Hiz; but towards Ippolyts brook the slope is more gradual, and the brick yards are placed in a valley-like depression which runs nearly at right angles to the direction of the ridge.

The brick earth, which is of course the *raison d'être* of the brick yards, is of a red brown colour, without perceptible stratification in the clay itself, but there occur layers in which small angular flints are very abundant, and these show plainly where after the digging the sides of the pits are left to the action of the weather. Besides these small flints, which are also sparsely scattered through the clay, there are comparatively few large stones in the brick earth.

The brick works commence just below Hitchin cemetery, about two-thirds of the distance from the brook to the summit of the ridge. Descending the ridge by the footpath (Taylor's Hill), which leads to the Folly, the first excavations will be seen on the right and left (Messrs. Ransom's pits), immediately after crossing Brick-kiln Lane.

It will be noticed that the clay has been dug here to a depth of 25ft. Proceeding down the path towards the Folly, pits from which clay has been dug occur on either side for some distance, but they terminate in the small allotment gardens in the rear of the cottages at the Folly.

Crossing the Stevenage Road, clay has again been dug at Mr. Jeeves's brick works. Here, however, it is only 3ft. to 6ft. thick, and looking back from this point, it will be noted that the brick earth thickens along the sides of the valley, and towards the ridge in proportion to the gradual rise of the ground.

Throughout this area the depth to which the clay is dug is governed by a bed of curious character. This is a calcareous loam of a pale yellow ochreous colour, sometimes almost white at the top. Its thickness at Mr. Jeeves's brick yards, where it can be seen to be underlain by some very coarse gravel, is about 8ft., but in another part of the same yard, more to the west, the yellow loam passes down into a blackish earth - unquestionably the same deposit, from its fossil contents. This was dug to 12ft. or 14ft., without getting to the bottom. A well which was dug some years ago in Mr. A. Ransom's pit penetrated similar material, without going through it. There is hardly any doubt that in an east-west direction the bed is practically level. Its surface is now exceedingly uneven and is broken into rounded bosses or hummocks between which is very tenacious brown clay. This irregular surface may be due partly perhaps, if not altogether, to the decalcification of the loam. That is to say, percolating water charged with humus or other acid dissolves the lime and carries it away in solution, leaving the clay as a residue.

That this goes on to a certain extent is unquestionable, for isolated patches of the loam may be found surrounded by clay, the edges of the patch showing the gradual passage of the loam to clay; there is not much doubt the clay immediately overlying the loam is the result of such decalcification...

I am not qualified to comment on the accuracy of Hill's conclusions. Perhaps there is a reader out there who might know. If so, let me know and I will provide you with a copy of the whole piece.

Simon Walker

Volume 14 no 2, October 2004

[The September issue of the same Journal printed a short article by Frank Latchmore on archaeology in the area.]

Hitchin and District Archaeology, 1891:
Antiquarian Notes

An interesting paper recently appeared in the *Herts. Express* (by a St. Albans clergyman) on "The six hills at Stevenage." The writer seems to have arrived at the conclusion that they are of Roman origin, from the finding of a portion of iron at the time one of them was opened.[1] It is very difficult to fix upon the date of the numerous earth-works and tumuli which occur in our neighbourhood. In several which have been excavated near Hitchin, evidence of at least two distinct interments have been noticed, and probably if the barrows had been properly opened, below the surface of the ground around, an interment of a much earlier period would have been found. In the early part of the present century a number of skeletons were found on the hill side looking over the village of Pirton. They were buried in a trench in rows, but no weapons or ornaments were found with the bodies to determine their nationality. A legend exists in Pirton that about this spot a sanguinary engagement was fought between the Danes (who seem to have been encamped near Pirton) and the Britons.

---

[1] The Six Hills are indeed of Roman origin. To quote from the Historic England website: " `The Six Hills' are impressive earthwork features and form the largest surviving group of burial mounds dating to the Roman period in England."

The former (the tradition says) were badly beaten and driven away. The quarrel originated (so my informant told me) in the attentions paid by the Danish soldiers to the British maidens, which provoked the wrath of their sweethearts. This is about the only tradition I have met with while prosecuting my antiquarian researches for many miles round the town of Hitchin. This is the more remarkable, as we are situated near one of the great streets or roads which intersect Britain. A large population must (by the traces we constantly find) have lived upon the hills and in the valley, watered by the river Hiz. Beyond the fact of several fields bearing the names of Long Dane, Short Dane, and Danesbury, history and tradition are silent as to the presence of Saxon and Dane, who perhaps after years of warfare settled down quietly with the native, and from whom many of us are descended. Some years ago a fine bronze torque or neck ornament was found near Pegsdon, round the neck of a skeleton interred at full length, beyond this (which no doubt was Celtic) nothing is known of the history of the whitened bones which lie in numbers hardly beneath reach of the plough, on the Chalk Hills of our township. Most of the Tumuli here have a local name; some of the names end with the old English term for hill, which is either Knoll or Hloe, or sometimes Hoo and Hoe. The principal barrows with names attached are Cainhoe, near Silsoe, the Money Knoll, near Pirton, Knockem Knoll to the right of the Cambridge line at Willbury Hill, Chalkman's Knoll also must have been the site of a tumulus, situated as it is on the summit of the hill near Ashwell, in a very commanding position. Limloe Hill, near Royston, was the largest in the locality, but it has unfortunately been lately removed bodily and strewn about the surrounding fields. I have carefully watched the process of destruction of this ancient relic in order to find some clue to its origin. It had, however, been previously rifled by treasure seekers and the interment (which was below the surface of the ground and not in the mound) removed or destroyed. Several small Celtic fibulæ were discovered, and on the top numerous Roman bronze coins of an early date. One of second brass of Titus with the very interesting reverse of Judea Capta is worthy of mention.

12th Sept., 1891.   FRANK LATCHMORE

Volume 14 no 2, October 2004

[The following piece was a short extract from a fireman's journal that my friend Dave Chalkley lent to me. I took the opportunity to copy it (with his permission), including the photographs and newspaper cuttings. Spellings are as per original. SLW]

Journal of a Fireman

1929
Fire at Lilly : on Wed Feb 13 a call was received by Phone about 11-0 am that a fire had broken out at Dog Kennel Farm owned by Mr. F. Allingham father of Fireman D Allingham. The Brigade turned out with motor pump and steamer on arrival found stacks well ablaze with Luton at work got Guy *[Morris Guy engine]* to work from Pond were the ice 3" thick

had to be Broken soon had a got *[good]* jet in the meantime the steamer had to be brought home as ice was on the tank. Luton returned home at 2.30 leaving Hitchin in charge but as the hose and motor got frozen up had to bring it home at 3 am Thursday the hose being so solid Block of ice had to be fetch home by motor lorry and had to be thawed by Fire Devils in the market this is one of the coldest fire attended by the H.F.B. Present Chief Officer D Powell 2 officer J Garratt F Fisher C Morris H Cannon J Valentine F Abbiss C/R French D Allingham H Sale.

Above: believed to be the haystack fire at Dog Kennel Farm, Lilly, on 13th February 1929. The hoses later froze solid. (David Chalkley)

*[The diary has several such accounts, as well as some photographs taken at the scene of the fires. Copying the diary turned out to be a good move, as Phil Howard, in conjunction with Hitchin Historical Society, produced a book based upon it (*Fire! Fire! Fireman Fisher's Hitchin Diary, 1926-1929*, 2014, ISBN: 978-0-9926162-1-2); Phil and members of the production team were thus able to work from a digital version, and not put any more wear and tear on the original. Phil's book is available from the Society.]*

Burgess Books

We at Burgess Books were always happy at the prospect of a new book coming from H.H.S. It would always be a boost to trade and if, as often happened, publication was set for October/November, it was good to know there would be a strong local title to sell for Christmas.

I think our association with Mrs Douglas began when she published 'The School on the Hill' and from then on we always became involved with her projects. We were pleased to have author-signings, which always proved very popular with the public, drawn by the splendid window displays the Society kindly provided at launch time. These were always so well done, complete with old photographs, artefacts, and documents etc. that we often had enquiries from customers who not only wanted to buy the book (at least in most cases!) they also wanted the old chimney pot, teddy bear or croquet mallet from the window display.

Sometimes there were doubts when you heard what the Society's next book was going to be about…. "Drains? Fishmongers? They'll never sell!", but, of course, they always pulled it off. No matter how long one has been in the book trade, the excitement of seeing a new book for the first time never wears off and it was always entertaining to hear a browser suddenly spot a photo of their granddad or old school friend, or themselves, in a local book. It was also pleasing when someone who had started with an Historical Society book then went on to publish their own titles, or were taken up by other publishers, and progressed from there. Many of your members were also regular and supportive customers and became friends – it was always a great pleasure to deal with you all.

By the very nature of its business, a bookshop is always interesting – you can never tell what the next enquiry is going to be. Customers' interest covers dozens of different subjects – it's definitely an insight into the catholic taste and downright quirkiness of people. Beekeeping, bell ringing, collecting all manner of articles, old steam trains (especially old steam trains!), there is a vast audience out there. We know all our regular customers' interests, so would let them know of any forthcoming title in their special subjects, be it volcanoes, tractors or fungi. I used to enjoy trying to predict what someone would be looking for as they walked in – 'there's a science fiction fan' (tattoos, beard, leather jacket)… 'Here's a mind – body – spirit aficionado' (lots of positive energy), 'here's someone who has forgotten his wife's birthday is today – she'll get a cookery book.' Of course, I was often wrong – people are not always so predictable – sometimes the gentlest, mildest old ladies were looking for murders – the gorier the better!

Above: Those were the days… Burgess Books' window, promoting the reprint of Discovering Hitchin, first published in October 1995, but here, in May 1996, 'back by popular demand'. Left, Pauline Humphries, Hitchin Historical Society's Publications Officer, and right, bookshop owner, Ann Barrington. [Scilla Douglas]

We also had our share of shoplifters; some of these were regulars too. It isn't easy to spot them in the act, but when you do, it makes you so angry you probably aren't as cautious as you should be. I saw one man put a book down the front of his trousers and shouted at him until he replaced it on the shelf. Luckily whoever bought it had no idea where it had been! There are people about who have no compunction about stealing charity boxes from the counter. On one occasion we had a publisher's sales representative in the shop at the time and he went looking for the thief who had thrown the collecting box into the hedge and pocketed the contents. The rep chased him, grabbed hold of his jacket and held tight. The thief got away but the rep returned with the pocket lining, full of coppers, having wrenched it off the jacket – never a dull moment!

We also seemed to attract all the local eccentrics – known in the trade as 'the bobble hat brigade' – one man told us so seriously that the Government was going to 'phase out white cars' that for a while we were convinced it was so. Or someone would say, 'I was in your shop two years ago, you had a book in that corner, I can't quite remember what it was called, but I think it had a blue cover and lovely illustrations, now I can't find it!'

Because 'the customer is always right' we couldn't argue, so some conversations were quite odd. "I want 'Of Mice and Men', please by William Shakespeare". "We've got 'Of Mice and Men' but it's by John Steinbeck". "No, I said I want the Shakespeare one." Or, "I've seen this book – it's published by Dolland and Aitchison – you've obviously never heard of them!" "I have, but I thought they were opticians – I think it's published by Dorling Kindersley." "That's what I meant."

A fascinating aspect of bookselling is that you are aware, often many months in advance, of a forthcoming event or trend. I remember a sales rep from Macmillan saying, "This book is going to shake the country and the Royal Family to the core" and believed this just to be publisher's pre-sale 'hype'. The book in question was Princess Diana's revelations about the marriage, courtesy of Anthony Holden, and the rest is history... I also remember the setting up of Bloomsbury Publishing – their list initially contained adult titles only, until one day their rep said,

> "We thought we'd have a go at children's books – just to see how they go" and they produced a proof copy of the first Harry Potter title. It was fun to try and spot the next title which would be a best seller, (often in December), a small quirky volume; for example, 'Schott's Original Miscellany' would be the one.

Over the years I had the privilege, either at book signings or publishers' launches, to meet various authors, among them Maeve Binchy, Danny Absie, John Hegley, Sarah Harrison, Colin Dexter, Gordon Beningfield, Victoria Glendinning, Michael Foreman, and for me, best of all, Joyce Grenfell.

So although my time in the Book Trade did not, unfortunately, have a traditional happy ending – I have many happy memories.

Ann Barrington

[When I was a child in the 1940s and '50s, I spent many happy hours browsing in the best shop in Bancroft. Birthday and Christmas book tokens were exchanged in Burgess Books, which was situated at No.108. As this small boy entered the long shop, it was like being transported into another world. The seemingly endless grey lino, with its characteristic aroma, led one past the pens and typewriters on the right and the cards and stationery on the left. The route went past the silent acolytes, counting their string and bulldog clips and led into the sanctum sanctorum presided over by the bespectacled avuncular figure of Mr Taylor and his respectably pearled wife. Silence reigned in this shrine to literacy, broken only by the tortured strains of piano playing from the music school above. This is where I learned to love books, especially those published by Collins, since they had the best smell...and glossy paper too!

The company was founded in the 1930s by a Mr Burgess and traded as a bookshop in Bancroft, changing hands on numerous occasions. It moved to its Churchyard location in the

1960s. At this time it was the only bookshop in the town and therefore a thriving business was conducted here with school and library supplies being effected from upstairs. Ann Barrington, the company's last director, joined the firm in 1974, and purchased it from Mr Halliday in 1989. Derek Wheeler]

Volume 16 no. 2, October 2006

Hitchin Girls' Club

Brian Worbey

Here is a good Hitchin quiz question. 'Where was Faggot Corner?'

However, more of that later. At an Historical Society meeting I was asked where was the Hitchin Girls' Club. Miss Aillie Latchmore founded the club in 1915 in a small room in the old Queen Street. It was formed specifically to give interests and hobbies to the young girls of the poor locality. Demolition of that street in the 1920s resulted in the club moving to Bethel Lane, opening in 1926. It was situated in a large wooden building with a committee room, kitchen, large open area, and stage with two changing rooms and, of course, toilets. Later a tennis court was added at the rear of the building.

Bethel Lane became St. John's Road after the Second World War and the club became Hitchin Clubland and around this time boys were becoming more and more involved in the club membership.

With support from Hertfordshire County Council the club was a great success, with over three hundred members at one time. So many groups were started within the club, country dancing and gymnastics, keep fit classes, singing, hand bell ringing, cookery, badminton, table tennis, football and the Sunday School. The list was almost endless!

Sadly, however, in the mid to late 1960s the club had to close as the County Council could no longer keep funding repairs to the building which had been targeted by continuous vandalism and damage. The club was put up for auction. Bids were put in by some of the participating groups as they wished to form a new club. However, they were ironically outbid by Hertfordshire County Council who eventually pulled down the club building as they wished to put in an extra access road for the new Fire and Ambulance Station in Newton's Way. The ambulance team later moved to Letchworth Gate and the road has never been built.

This brings me back to Faggot Corner! At the end of Pulters Way, where it leads into St. John's Road, there is a fenced in open ground alongside the cemetery wall. Here is a detached, private house. This was built as a butchers and general store in 1926 for Joe Day and his family who had also moved from Queen Street. Joe Day was famous in the 20s, 30s, and 40s for black puddings sourced from Grundens in Shillington, pease pudding and, of course, <u>hot faggots!</u>

Volume 16 no. 1, February 2006

Derek Wheeler provided the following report from the early days of the first World War:

November 26th 1914

An Awkward Customer in Queen Street

Petty Sessions: John Wilson (40) labourer.

P.C. Webb stationed at Hitchin said he was on duty in Queen Street about 9.50 p.m. when he heard a crash of broken glass. He proceeded to the 'Bricklayers Arms' and there saw the defendant in a very excited condition, walking away and using very threatening language. He brought him to the police station. Defendant was drunk, but not incapable and very excited. Defendant said that he had a little drink. Supt. Reed said he was a stranger to the district. Ordered to pay 5s. damages and a fine of 5s. for refusing to quit the premises, and 7s. 6d. costs – 17s. 6d. in all, or 7 days.

 (Readers may be interested to learn that in amongst the treasures which are held in the Museum Store is an iron handcart, which is painted green. This trusty vehicle is the one upon which the drunks were conveyed to the old police station in Bancroft. It has seen better days, since it has a rather drunken appearance itself at present. Many years ago when the Museum Store was in the old Fire Station in Paynes Park, a hit-and-run motorcyclist tried to ride his machine through the closed doors of the fire station and came to rest against one of the wheels of the cart. The fate of the motorcyclist has yet to be researched! Ed.)

(I can tell you, Derek: he was an acquaintance of mine. He survived the accident, but suffered serious scaring to his face. Simon Walker)

Volume 18 no. 2, October 2008

Stained Glass Panels in Hermitage Road

Simon Walker

   At the lower end of Hermitage Road, on the north side, is a three-storey building, put up when that side of the road was developed for retail at the end of the 1920s. It stands on the corner once occupied by the Hermitage, a converted 16th century barn (with 18th century additions). The house was occupied by, amongst others, William Wilshere, John Ransom (who had a flour and corn mill in the front room), Mary Exton (his daughter) and Mary-Ann Exton, his granddaughter; she married Frederic Seebohm – the man who donated the land for the construction of Hermitage Road in 1874.[1]

Above: On the right (Abbott and Son) is the building housing the window with the stained glass panels. They are just visible on the first floor in this postcard dating from the 1930s (Gerry Tidy).

Above the entrance to the shop – at the time of writing unoccupied, but previously Abbott and Son, Clement Joscelyne and Wallace Kings – on the first floor is a window, and it is this window that is the subject of this article.

At first glance, the window seemed much like all the others, but if you looked closely, you will see that it has several – six, in fact – stained glass panels set into it. What were they, and how did they come to be there?

We shall be looking at the window in the way it was best viewed, from the inside. Thus the top left from the inside is the top right if you're standing in the street.

The panels are of at least two different periods and origins, possibly more; they do not therefore belong together, but have been assembled at a later date.

---

[1] Helen Poole & Alan Fleck, *Old Hitchin, Portrait of an English Market Town*, Eric T Moore, (1976), p.p. 39 & 44.

Above: The window, showing the six stained glass panels.[1]

Four are roundels depicting religious icons; one is an armorial bearing (a coat of arms, in popular parlance); and one is – well, at the moment it's a puzzle. The roundels and the armorial bearing are single pieces of glass; the final panel consists of two pieces. Let's start with the religious icons.

The Religious Roundels

All four date from the first quarter of the sixteenth century (c.1525), and are of Flemish origin. These were made in large numbers in the Low Countries between the fifteenth and

---

[1] All photographs of the window were taken by the author. If in some cases they seem to be from an odd angle, it is because they were taken where possible with a background of the sky, rather than the buildings opposite. I would like to thank the management and staff of Clement Joscelyne for their kind co-operation and assistance.

seventeenth centuries. They were painted with yellow (silver) stain and black/brown glass-paint. Later, from the seventeenth century onwards, enamel colours were introduced.[1]

Image 1: Top left, the Resurrection

The colours are black/brown and yellow. This image is a depiction of the resurrection of Christ: the sarcophagus lid is pushed to one side, and the Christ figure (with His head surrounded by a halo) is shown stepping out. He carries a staff, topped with a cross. The Roman guards lie sleeping around Him. They are shown in mediæval armour; this is quite common for the period, when historical accuracy of costume was widely ignored, either deliberately or through ignorance of how soldiers of earlier ages were equipped.

---

[1] *Vidimus*, no 14, *Roundels of Light*, January 2008:
http://www.vidimus.org/archive/issue_14_2008/issue_14_2008-01.html (accessed 17 April 2008).

There are similarities between this image and a panel pained by Hans Memling (1430? – 1495), a Flemish artist; it is a standard icon, widely found.

Above: Hans Memling's version of the resurrection of Christ, c.1490, now in the Louvre, Paris. Note the mediæval armour of the sleeping guards. (Public domain image)

Image 2: Top right, The Archangel St Michael and Satan

This roundel is damaged; I believe it was caused by a window cleaner's ladder. The panels are now protected by a plastic shield.

At first sight, this image seems to shout, "St George and the dragon!" But it's not. There are a number of rules and guidelines for differentiating between the two:[1]

- St George is usually mounted on horseback; St Michael is not
- St George wears a cross symbolising him as a Christian knight; St Michael does not
- St Michael does not always wear armour; George always does
- St Michael tramples Satan underfoot; St George's horse tramples the dragon
- St Michael sometimes carries a book or scales; George never does
- Background scenes might also provide clues

---

[1] I am much indebted to Roger Rosewell of Vidimus for his patience and assistance in this identification, especially in the face of my insistence that it looked like St George to me!

In addition, we have to remember that in the Low Countries, St George did not carry the same significance he did in Britain.

Bearing all this in mind, let's look at the roundel. It is black, brown and yellow, like the resurrection roundel, and is of a similar date (c. 1525). A knight figure, on foot, thrusts a broken lance into the throat, and through the back of the head of, a clawed and tailed creature with a formidable set of teeth.

Although Satan is often shown in human form in depictions of St Michael, the dragon form is not unusual. According to the Revelation of St John, "...there was war in heaven: Michael and his angels fought against the dragon; and the dragon fought and his angels. And prevailed not, and neither was their place found any more in heaven. And the great dragon was cast out, that old serpent, called the Devil, and Satan..."[1]

In the knight's right hand he holds a broadsword above his head, ready to strike. He carries nothing else, and wears no cross. There seem to be no clues in the background that help us, unfortunately.

There is no doubt that here we have St Michael. He fits all the criteria bar the last two, and they are optional. The armour is similar to that of some of the sleeping soldiers in the Resurrection roundel, even to the extent that there is a yellow band at the base of the chain mail, and yellow-tinted besagews.[2] Are the two panels perhaps by the same painter?

There has been some damage to this panel and roundel in recent years; the roundel itself has a crack across it (difficult to see in this photograph), and the supporting glass on the right is splintered. None of this damage is apparent in photographs displayed on the CVMA (Corpus Vitrearum Medii Aevi) website in their survey of medieval glass.[3]

Image 3: Bottom left, the visitation of Elizabeth by the Virgin Mary

Unlike the first two, there is a distinctly brown tinge to the painting of the third roundel, and the trees in the background are different in style, suggesting a different artist. There are no clues in the background, which consists of hills with the occasional tree. Two figures are depicted, both pregnant women; both have halos. The Virgin Mary, on the left, is bare-headed, with her hair loose (a symbol of virginity). The other figure has a hand on the abdomen of the first, feeling for the child in the womb. This is Elizabeth, mother of John the Baptist. According to Luke 1:36-56, Elizabeth was Mary's cousin.

---

[1] Revelation of St John the Divine, 12, 7-9.

[2] A *besagew* is a round piece of body armour designed to protect a joint of the body, often, as in this case, the armpit. From the Old French, a two-edged axe.

[3] The CVMA website was **http://www.cvma.ac.uk/index.htm** (accessed 8 May 2008 but no longer active).

Above: the visitation of Elizabeth by the Virgin Mary.

Left: The visitation from a missal from Flanders, dating from 1525-50, pretty close to the date of the roundel. It bears features in common with the glass image, including a bare-headed Virgin Mary and the pregnancy of both women, especially Mary, who stands on the right. (Free Library of Philadelphia, Item No. mca1571861, Folio f. 186r)

Image 4: Bottom right, St Nicholas Reanimates Three Murdered Children

St. Nicholas, a fourth century Bishop of Myra, in Turkey, is the Patron of bakers, pawnbrokers, sailors, children, Greeks and Russians; his Feast day is December 6th.

The companion of St. Nicholas, Père Fouettard, is said to be the butcher of three children, whom he pickled in a brine-tub. The saint discovered the murder, and resurrected the three children. It is this tale that is depicted in the roundel.

It seems that the whole story may be based on a misinterpretation. According to a ninth century history of the saint, a citizen of Patara had lost all his money, and, because of his poverty, was unable to provide dowries for his three daughters; as a result, he intended that they should become prostitutes. The wealthy St Nicholas, hearing of this, provided anonymous dowries, contained in purses, for all three girls.[1] It was representations of the

---

[1] This is the source of the tradition of the giving of gifts by St Nicholas. Père Fouettard is also called the whip father, because he whips naughty children. This tradition is continued in a somewhat sanitized form as the withholding of gifts from them. Not in the same league as punishments go.

purses, which came to be mistaken for the heads of three children, that gave rise to the story of the resuscitated children.[1]

Left: St Nicholas and the three children as depicted in a Flemish Book of Hours, c.1484-1529. (MS 7, 209r, Special Collections Research Center, Syracuse University Library)

Whatever the truth might be, by the Middle Ages the story of the three children had become firmly established, and the iconography fixed. St Nicholas is depicted with halo, mitre and crosier, dressed in contemporary religious robes; he is blessing the three children, who stand, naked, in the brine tub in which they have been pickled.

The roundel is Flemish, and dates from the same period as images 1 to 3. It is black/brown and yellow. It is stylistically similar to the others, especially to image 3.

---

[1] *Lives of the Saints: With Excerpts from Their Writings*, John J. Crawley and Co., Inc., (1954).

The Secular Panels
Image 5: Centre left, Rose and Crown

At present this panel is something of a mystery. At first sight, I thought that this panel was a depiction of the top of a robed head, with a crown above it. Closer examination makes it quite clear that the lower element is a rose.

Presumably there was once a lower half to the rose, but we don't know that for sure; its age is uncertain; it's not even certain that the two elements – the rose and the crown – share a common origin. The rose has five inner and five outer petals, the regulation layout for an heraldic rose. The crown has alternate fleurs-de-lys and crosses, four of each. Above the crown, supported by gold bands, is an orb and cross. It seems to be a crown of the King of England.[1]

Assuming that the two elements belong together, we have several interpretations.[2]

The first is most commonly associated with public houses (we have a Rose and Crown in the Marketplace here in Hitchin, of course).

> "Like most pub signs this one had its origins in the Middle Ages when it was associated with the cult of the Virgin Mary (which arrived in this country in the 12th century) - she being referred to both as the Rosa Mundi (the Rose of the World) and the Queen of Heaven..."[3]

Could the glass have come from an inn? It's possible. Could it have come from a church, or other religious institution, associated in some way with the cult of the Virgin Mary? Again, possible.

It could be that there is an heraldic explanation, in the form of a badge:

> A distinctive mark worn by servants, retainers, and followers of royalty or nobility, who, being beneath the rank of gentlemen, have no right to armorial bearings. The rose and crown is the badge of the servants, &c., of the Kings of England...[4]

It might be that the panel originated from the establishment of a servant to the crown, but I have no evidence other than its appearance to support such a supposition – the rose is of the right type, as is the crown.

It is asserted that the origins of the emblem lie in the Wars of the Roses:

> The frequency of the rose as a vintner's sign had its origin in the adoption of the red rose of Lancaster, or the white rose of York, by the several adherents of those factions. The marriage of the Lancastrian King Henry the Seventh with Elizabeth of York extinguished the feuds which the rivalry of these royal houses had created; and the Tudor rose, half red, half white, surmounted by the crown, became the royal badge, and as a sign, designated " the rose and

---

[1] Grant, Francis J., *The Manual of Heraldry; Being a Concise Description of the Several Terms Used, and Containing a Dictionary of Every Designation in the Science* (fifth edition), Arthur Hall, Virtue & Co., p.67.

[2] Much of what follows is speculation, though not without foundation.

[3] *The Temples of John Barleycorn*, Whitedragon website, http://www.whitedragon.org.uk/articles/john.htm (accessed 22 April 2008).

[4] Grant, Francis J., *The Manual of Heraldry*, p.50.

crown;" while the semi-colours became in time unused, their origin and meaning being imperfectly understood.[1]

Left: the rose and crown badge, as it appears in the Manual of Heraldry, *c.1880.*

This could well be true, though it sounds a little romantic, with an odour of the "Merrie England" beloved of the Victorians.

The observant reader will have noticed that the rose and crown emblem is still in use; next time you handle a twenty pence piece, look at the reverse.

Which, if any, is the correct solution? In truth, I don't know. If I had to guess? I think the panel probably came from either a wealthy household, a member of which at one time had a

---

[1] Jacob Henry Burn, *Descriptive Catalogue of the London Traders, Tavern, and Coffee-House Tokens Current in the Seventeenth Century,*1855, p.35. Digitized by Google.
https://tinyurl.com/4hhhy9w

connection with the crown; or a public house. But these are is no more than guesses, and I wouldn't care to lay money on them.

Image 6: Centre right, the Armorial Bearing

Let me start by admitting that I am not an expert on heraldry, so I offer the following with some reservations.

The panel has been reversed within the last few years. It used to face to the right, which meant that the motto at the bottom was reversed when viewed from within the building. This has now been corrected, though I don't know by whom, nor exactly when.

David White, a herald of the College of Arms, has identified the bearing, and reports it as being the arms and crest by Abraham Wildey Robarts of 26 Hill Street, Berkeley Square, London and Besborough House, Roehampton, Surrey who died in 1858. His report runs as follows:

The arms in the glass may be blazoned (tinctures uncertain). **Three Crossbows**, and the crest, on a wreath Gules[1] (?) and Argent[2], **Upon a Mount Vert[3] a Stag lodged proper reguardant attired Or[4]**. In heraldry the helm, and usually any animal or monster in the crest face, to the viewer's left so in the image you sent the arms are clearly the wrong way round. I imagine they are intended to be seen from the other side.

This combination of arms and crest could not be found in our official records of arms granted and confirmed by the English Kings of Arms, but was found in an unofficial compilation of arms, *Burke's General Armory*, last edition 1884. They are there described as **Argent three Crossbows, two and one** and the crest, **A stag lodged proper attired Or...**

Despite minor differences in the description and the glass image, he is "confident that the same arms are meant. In Burke these are attributed to Robarts of Hill Street, Berkeley Square, London."

Mr White adds that the *London Post office Directory* for 1847 gives under Robarts, "Robarts, Abraham, esq. 26 Hill St. & Besborough House, Roehampton." In addition, he sent information from the *Oxford Dictionary of National Biography* for the Robarts family and for Abraham Wildey Robarts (1779-1858) who lived and died at 26 Hill Street. [5]

Though the motto is degraded, close inspection reveals it to be *Legendo & Scribendo (by reading and writing;* not one of the most inspiring of legends). According to the *Oxford Dictionary of National Biography*, the Robarts family were successful bankers, who came to prominence with Abraham Robarts (1745-1816), father of Abraham Wildey Robarts.

During our investigations into the Robarts family,[6] a second example of the Robarts bearing came to light on a bookplate in a set of bound dictionaries that once belonged to the Robarts family. In this case there can be no doubt as to whom this bearing belongs – it has his name printed beneath it.

---

[1] Gules = red.
[2] Argent = silver or white.
[3] Vert = green.
[4] Or = gold.
[5] Reply from D. V. White, Somerset Herald, College of Arms, Queen Victoria Street, London, dated 22 March 2008.
[6] By "our" I mean predominantly Zena Grant. Zena is a professional researcher, and once she gets started there is no stopping her. I am deeply obliged for all her efforts, and I wish I could include all the information she dug up.

Left: The arms that appear in the bound volumes of "A General Dictionary, Historical and Critical: in which a new and accurate translation of that of the celebrated Mr Bayle, with the Corrections & Observations Printed in the Late Edition at Paris, included..." The books were published in 1734, but the bookplates may well be a good deal later. (By kind permission of Michael Kousah of Ely Books (Elybooks.com))

The College of Arms response to the bookplate was as follows:

> The bookplate shows the arms quartered and impaled and they are consistent with belonging to the same man. The showing of quarterings and of one's wife's arms in an impalement are not compulsory and it is quite normal to use the simple version of one's arms as well as or instead of the more complicated version.
>
> I should add that it is possible that the window is intended to be the arms of AWR's father.

The printed arms have several features in common with the glass panel; the stag "lodged proper regardant," and the crossbows two and one (two above, one below).

The other features are not so easy to account for. Robarts married a Charlotte Wilkinson in 1808; the Wilkinson bearing includes unicorns; so it may be that the printed example follows the marriage. Is the glass the arms of the earlier Abraham Robarts? As with the Rose and Crown, we don't know.

The Origins of the Window

We know that the window was once in the Hermitage itself, because a manuscript by Frank Hoyland, written in the 1930s, refers to it:

> ...in 1929 the whole of the Seebohm property was sold for building purposes... Several of the boys may remember that the staircase window in the Hermitage had three [sic] decorations in Stained glass. When this window was taken down, along with the rest of this beautiful building, these were carefully preserved, and they are now fixed in the first floor angle window of the new buildings, at the corner of Bancroft and Hermitage Road. They are unfortunately too high to be properly seen from the street level, but I have been able to recognize them in passing, from the top of an Eastern National Bus![1]

Though Mr Hoyland says that there were only "three decorations in Stained glass" it is highly likely that he is talking about the same window – he says he recognise "them". The discrepancy in numbers might be accounted for by a lapse in memory; or perhaps the panels were mounted in a different layout when he was a boy. We do not know for certain that the panels were all in a single window when they were in the Hermitage; we do not even know whether they formed a group at that time. It is possible that they were assembled as they appear now when they were installed in their current location. Certainly, the window into which they are now set fits remarkably well in size and style to the others in the building.

It seems likely to me, though, that the Flemish roundels at least formed a group in the Hermitage. Such roundels were collected in this country in the 19th century, and it seems reasonable to suppose that these examples form such a collection.

As for the Rose & Crown, it is possible that it formed part of a window in the old Rose and Crown pub in the Market Place; the original building, which had been a pub since the 18th century, was demolished in around 1935, and rebuilt as we see it today.[2] Could the glass have been rescued from there, and included in the window when it was moved in 1929? Perhaps, though I doubt it – the dates don't match.

And then we have the Robarts armorial bearing. Abraham Wildey Robarts' brother, William, was MP for St Albans from 1818. Is the stag on the bearing in fact a hart, so well known as the county symbol?

---

[1] Frank Frazer Hoyland, *Reminiscences of a Hitchin School In the 1870's and 1880's*, a facsimile of a 1935 manuscript, published by Hitchin Historical Society, 2002, p.p.32-33.

[2] Alan Fleck, *Exploring Hitchin*, a CD published by Hitchin Historical Society, 2006.

The Robarts family were bankers, as were several of the leading citizens of Hitchin, Frederic Seebohm included. Might the glass have reached the Hermitage as a result of some such link? For now, that's where we have to leave it.

Where is the Window Now?

I contacted Hitchin Property Trust, the owner of the building. Stephen Carter was most helpful:

> Due to the residential conversion works above the old furniture shop the stained glass window on the first floor was removed. We appreciate its significance and we arranged for the careful donation of the glass to the Hitchin Museum. The original windows and frames across the building were in such a poor state that we had to replace them all with modern energy efficient counterparts and new oak subframes, all to replicate the existing design. We did previously have the window in question covered inside and out with perspex to prevent any accidental or malicious damage but this would not have been allowed to stay as this room will now be a bedroom and it needs to open for ventilation and egress in the event of a fire.

The panels were passed, via Tom Hardy, the Town Centre Manager, to North Hertfordshire Museum; it is their intention to display them.

Above: every so often a picture turns up we can't identify. I'm told that this is in Hitchin, but where? If you know, we'd be delighted to hear from you... (SLW)

Postscript

I'm afraid that's all we have room for in this volume. I hope you find it as interesting as the first – if you haven't got a copy, you'd better hurry.

There is plenty more material though, enough for another three volumes after this, and I hope we'll be publishing it in 2020, in time for Christmas that year – the ideal gift for the historically minded. If that sounds like a plug, that's because it is!

The Hitchin Journal was, and still is, printed in black and white, and where possible I've tried to source colour images. Sometimes of course there ARE no colour images, especially of older photographs. The article about the stained glass panels (pages 164-181) is a perfect example. All the images were converted to monochrome when the article was published. Fortunately I kept the originals, and was able to replace boring old black and white with the original colour images.

There have been, and will be, cases where further research has thrown new light on some articles, and these have been corrected. If you find something that you believe to be incorrect, please contact the Society via its website:

http://www.hitchinhistoricals.org.uk/

If you'd like to join the Society, you'll find details of how to do that on the website too. The subscription is what is often now referred to as "affordable" (cheap). There is lots of other interesting things on there too.

While we're on the subject of websites, references to online sources were correct at the time the articles were written; but the internet is ephemeral, and websites have a habit of disappearing. This is beyond our control, I'm afraid. I hope you enjoy the book.

Simon Walker

Left: history is all around us, some of it in material form. These three bullets (all have been fired) were found locally by a metal detectorist friend. They all date from the Second World War, and are, left to right, a .5in US bullet, a 7.92mm German bullet, and a .303 British bullet. What were they doing out in a field? We can only guess: the .303 and the .5in perhaps from a test firing of guns from an allied bomber or fighter on its way to continental Europe; the 7.92 from a German bomber or fighter, any time between 1940-45. (With thanks to Phil Kirk)

Index

Above: Hitchin Station, looking north-west, and showing the old limeworks in the foreground, now the station car park and a number of business units. Below: Hitchin goods siding and station. [SLW]